THE RELUCTANT ALLERGY EXPERT

HOW TO KILL THE FEAR THAT ANAPHYLAXIS COULD KILL YOU

By

Ruth Holroyd

The Reluctant Allergy Expert:
How to kill the fear that anaphylaxis could kill you

Edited by Sally Beck

Designed by Emma Nissé

Published in 2020 by Curlew Books

ISBN: 978-1-912798-16-2

Contents

Introduction

This book will give you the information you need to not only live with life-threatening allergies, but also to thrive, experience life to the full and enjoy every experience; because you shouldn't have to miss out. If you, or a loved one, is allergic to anything that can cause an anaphylactic reaction, you will know how terrifying living with that fear is.

I have pulled together lots of research and first-hand experience to help you learn how to come to terms with the diagnosis, and to bridge the gap between discovering you have this condition and finally adapting to enjoying your life without feeling depressed, anxious, fearful and excluded.

I hope this book will bring you help, support and, overall, positivity, to face this frightening condition with strength, confidence and assertiveness.

DISCLAIMER

The information contained in this book is not a substitute for a consultation with your own doctor. It should not take the place of professional medical advice in any way and should not be relied upon as such. It is designed to give you a base understanding of a health issue and provide pointers to help you.

Always check with your doctor or nutritionist before making any changes to your diet, medicines or supplements. Always exercise common sense. We accept no responsibility whatsoever for illness arising out of failure to seek medical advice from a doctor.

CHAPTER 1

MY ANAPHYLAXIS JOURNEY...

This is my story. It describes how I became a reluctant expert in anaphylaxis and allergies. It has been a long and difficult journey. If I could change anything about myself, it would be my atopic challenges with both allergies and eczema. If someone could wave a wand and give me no allergies and normal skin... that would be a miracle and my dream come true.

Eczema can sometimes be a sign of food allergies. For example, doctors think that my childhood eczema was caused by dairy. When I gave dairy up, my eczema went away for a short while so maybe they were right?

I often wonder what my life would have been like if I had not had these conditions. But living daily with life affecting and limiting conditions has taught me so much about myself. It has taught me strength and bravery; it has taught me empathy and sympathy. And most recently, it has taught me that I must turn kindness, empathy and understanding on myself because I have always held silent shame, guilt and loathing for my skin and allergy limitations.

Through my blog whatallergy.com, I have channelled my positivity to help others but neglected my own self-care. In the last few years, the anxiety and fear that overtook me helped me face up to these negative ways of thinking about myself.

I have learned so many tips and essential planning measures that keep me safe, and believe one hundred per cent that it is possible to live a full, active and inclusive life with serious allergies. But it takes organisation, practise and is a constant learning curve!

Join me on the allergic march to better understanding.

WHERE IT ALL BEGAN

As a child growing up in the 1970s and 1980s, I had bad eczema, hay fever and rhinitis – a constant runny nose. I was also allergic to cats, rabbits and dogs from an early age. This pained me greatly, and I was forever being told off for playing with Aunty Prue's guinea pigs, or for stroking the lovely little Westie that belonged to a friendly old man down our road. I always wanted a pet, but this dream was sadly not possible due to mine and my sister's animal allergies. But we did have goldfish, and feral hamsters due to not really being able to handle them!

Nothing was ever really done about my skin except emollients, starting with the worst ones which irritated my skin and of course, topical steroids. No doctor ever suggested allergies might be causing my skin problems. And for allergies, there was no treatment except antihistamine tablets, and these were expensive and not available on the NHS.

I can remember having an oral allergy syndrome (OAS) to apples, carrots and other fruits and vegetables. If I ate them, my lips itched and swelled up. Nothing else bad happened though so I grew up eating these foods and putting up with the unwelcome side effects; although I chose something else if there was a choice. OAS is not life-threatening and happens when foods cross-react with hay fever due to the body recognising the foods as similar to a pollen allergen that you are already allergic to.

Ignoring the first signs, as I had done here, proved very dangerous when it came to me suffering more severe food allergy reactions in later life. The first time I remember eating peanuts, I thought they tasted disgusting. My Mum said that as a small child I never liked them and would refuse to eat them, but no one knew just how bad this could get. No one foresaw that this could become life-threatening as food allergies were not really known about then.

Children can be picky and, overall, I was a healthy child and enjoyed most other foods with gusto. I ate like a horse! But even the smell of peanuts was horrible to me. Was this my body's early warning signal to protect itself and stop me consuming that particular food? I would get a tingling in my lips and a kind of shuddering feeling deep in my throat if I ate even a tiny trace of peanut.

Back then, a small exposure to nuts would be sort of okay. I would not feel great but if I stopped eating whatever it was and had an antihistamine, I could avoid a serious attack. If I managed to eat a whole peanut by mistake, I would be extremely ill. Our diet at home was healthy and basic, and we generally did not eat things that contained peanuts or nuts, so it was fairly easy for me to avoid them.

If I did eat nuts by mistake, over the years, the allergic reactions got worse. I became violently sick, and I mean projectile vomiting through my mouth, and, rather shockingly, through my nose. It took my Mum quite some time to work out what was making me so ill because kids are sick, sometimes for no apparent reason.

My Mum finally worked out what the problem was after piecing together the incidents. For instance, they often happened around Christmas, birthdays, or Easter, when I would inadvertently eat a Quality Street brazil nut chocolate or cake containing peanuts.

One horrible experience has always stayed with me. At school one day, when I was about 8 years old, lunch was a rather unappealing salad which had about six peanuts on the side. I did not eat them, and when the dinner lady questioned me, I told her they made me feel sick. She forced me to eat them, holding out one at a time, so being the polite, well-mannered little girl that I was, I obeyed her. I managed to eat about two before I promptly vomited all over the dining room floor, my shoes and the dinner lady's shoes. Far from being sympathetic, the dinner lady was really cross with me, even though my Mum had warned the school I could not eat nuts. I was a quiet, shy girl at school, and this gave me some small fame. The girl who puked on the dinner lady! I was cool! For once!

This would be unheard of now, and luckily, I survived that incident. It is great to see how far we have come since then. Most schools are very understanding and will handle nut, and other allergies, better than this dinner lady, who thought I was just being picky and leaving perfectly good food on my plate. Allergies just were not common back then and I was the only kid in a school of 200 children with a peanut allergy.

LEARNING THE HARD WAY ABOUT ANAPHYLAXIS

Things got harder as I got older and I remember suffering many reactions after eating out. I think my Mum knew something bad was happening to me because when I had a really bad reaction, I would go completely limp and motionless after the vomiting. I would go to bed exhausted and Mum would keep regularly waking me to check I was still breathing. I can remember being annoyed and wishing she would just let me sleep but a mother's instinct, when powerless to help, is to do what she can. Back then, you only called the doctor in a dire emergency and this was not considered an emergency. Sadly, all she could do was just watch and wait and pray it would all be okay.

My first bad anaphylactic reaction happened while I was at university in Buckinghamshire in 1992, age 19. I was on a work placement at a paper-making company in Beaconsfield, Buckinghamshire, so thankfully, was close to home. Me and my colleagues went to an Indian restaurant where I ordered a nut-free meal. It arrived with nuts! I sent it back and told them I was allergic to nuts – although I was not formally diagnosed until the following year – and would be really ill. I stressed that this was important, I needed a safe meal, or I would go without. They said they would do it for me without nuts but unfortunately, they decided to pick out as many nuts as they could and bring back the contaminated meal all smiles and assurances. I knew from the first mouthful that something was not right and then spotted a nut in the sauce.

I quickly became extremely ill in the restaurant. I began feeling sick and ran to the loo to throw up. The staff did not care and refused to speak to me afterwards and in fact told me not to come back again as they could not serve me. You can imagine this was scary, being out with friends who tried to look after me. Since the night was still young, they took me back to the flat where my then boyfriend lived, then went back out. When he got home, he found me passed out in bed with pools of vomit on the floor. The next day my airways and nostrils were almost closed shut and I was terrified. What had just happened to me?

That reaction scared me. Shortly after that, I heard of a young woman who died after eating peanuts. This happened in 1993 and she was just 17 years old, just a few years younger than I was at the time. Her name was Sarah Reading and she was a trainee hairdresser from Ash, near Aldershot in Hampshire. Sarah's grieving father, David Reading, wanting to make sense of his daughter's death, founded the Anaphylaxis Campaign (see Chapter 16 for details) to fund research and support, in an effort to prevent any further deaths due to allergies.

I now had to face the terrifying truth that this allergy had taken on a much more sinister air. This thing could be life-threatening? I had never faced that thought before and it shook me!

After that, I got a diagnosis – I was allergic to nuts. The advice from doctors then was simply to avoid nuts. There was no other treatment apart from antihistamine tablets, which did nothing for bad reactions. (Since then I have also become allergic to soya and dairy.)

This was in the early 1990s, before Google was founded in 1998. It is incredible to imagine a life without Google. It meant there was no easy way to research your condition then, which was not such a bad thing, because Dr Google can be quite scary.

Thankfully, I was finally prescribed adrenaline when I was age 26, which gave me some peace of mind. But the first adrenaline I ever had was a phial of the liquid drug and a syringe to inject it with. I was far too scared to use it.

One vivid memory from this time was when the nurse showed my Mum and I how to use the adrenaline and syringe. She opened the front buttons of her dress and demonstrated stabbing the syringe into her stomach. I was so shocked to see a woman's bare stomach exposed like that that I did not really pay any attention to the instructions that followed. I had never seen a woman's naked belly before. I probably stared very rudely as young people will.

"I'm not doing that! Ever!", I told my Mum.

Thankfully, we never did administer the adrenaline in this way as it was awful advice. The correct place to administer adrenaline is always into the side of the thigh. (Details of how to do this can be found in Chapter 7.)

Thank goodness we now have self-administering adrenaline autoinjectors.

The attacks just kept rolling on...

Over the years, I have had many anaphylactic attacks. I used to know how many I had had but I have now lost count. There are around 10 incidents where I have been hospitalised and another 30 where I have been on the point of using my adrenaline. This is despite me being very careful and always, always checking with restaurants and labels in supermarkets. Because mistakes happen. Too often.

Sometimes these mistakes have been my own fault. My first proper full-on anaphylactic reaction to dairy occurred because I did not know that this could even happen. I had cut dairy out of my diet because it gave me eczema, and it caused minor irritable bowel syndrome (IBS), but somewhere along the line I had developed anaphylaxis to it. This is proof that reactions that were once mild and inconvenient, can turn much, much worse without warning. So, I ordered scrambled eggs, mixed with cream and butter, in a lovely pub at the end of my road. I figured I would just suffer the sore skin that butter and milk might cause. I never knew that milk could cause me to suffer an anaphylactic reaction.

After I collapsed, to begin with I completely mistrusted the pub and assumed that I must have eaten nuts in the bread or that somehow, they had cross-contaminated my meal, but they had not, it was just a new reaction. As I dissected the meal with the staff, I realised that nuts were not the problem at all, but discovered that the scrambled eggs contained lots of butter and milk... could it have been this? Skin prick tests and blood tests at Amersham Hospital, Buckinghamshire, proved that I did indeed have a severe dairy allergy.

I also once famously had an allergic reaction to a sample given to me at the Allergy Show! A company made gluten and dairy-free macaroni cheese. I tried it and it was lovely, so I went back to get some more. They also had a full dairy version that they gave to me by mistake. At the Allergy Show, I had mistakenly felt that I was safe.

Due to this, and other reactions at the same show, big changes were made to regulations, training and labelling and they are now much safer places to be.

Every time I have a reaction, I like to feel that I use the situation to educate myself and others and put in place procedures and processes to ensure further mistakes are not made. But how many more will I survive? They have got so bad now that I wonder when I have one if it will be my last.

Age 47, I seem to have one serious reaction or near miss every year, which is not a good track record. These near misses have all happened whilst eating out, despite checking, double checking and triple checking, the restaurants still manage to serve me food that has caused anaphylaxis. These days, it is always dairy as this seems so much less understood and harder to avoid than nuts. My dairy allergy also now seems far more severe than my nut allergy.

Despite being unlucky, I refuse to lie down, stay home and give in. I want to enjoy life, to explore, learn new things and be part of this incredible, inspiring and amazing world we live in. My life now is a mission to educate and spread awareness of life-threatening allergies. We must stop avoidable, unnecessary deaths from anaphylaxis.

CHAPTER 2

THE PSYCHOLOGICAL IMPACT OF LIVING WITH ANAPHYLAXIS BY DR FRANCESCA SAWER

Dr Francesca Sawer, is the Highly Specialist Clinical Psychologist at Guy's and St Thomas' NHS Foundation Trust, Evelina Hospital Children's Allergy Service. She said:

> *Reading Ruth's story, for me, was a reminder of the narratives that I regularly hear working as a clinical psychologist with the children and families of young people living with life-threatening allergies. Whilst fortunately, not everyone with allergies will have experienced anaphylaxis in the way Ruth has, raising awareness of the psychological impact of anaphylaxis and those fearing such a reaction happening to them in the future, is something which I welcome getting more recognition. I believe that we have come a long way in the past few years in raising awareness of the psychological impact of living with allergies that Ruth discusses so well; however, we*

still have much further to go in getting parity in the treatment and support for the psychological consequences and issues associated with this.

Experiencing a serious allergic reaction can be traumatic, for those who experience it and for those who may witness it; for example parents, siblings, and friends. Just like Ruth's experience, we know that the after-effects can often be linked with an increase in anxiety, traumatic symptoms including flashbacks and nightmares, panic attacks and behaviours including withdrawal from social activities and avoidance of particular places or foods, in addition to increased hyper-vigilance around checking of food labels. We call these 'safety' behaviours because they are behaviours that help to make a person feel safe in the short term and therefore reduce immediate anxiety. However, long term may unfortunately serve to maintain anxiety and most of the time increase it, due to reduced opportunities to learn more effective strategies for managing and facing the trauma or anxiety.

As a clinical psychologist, my work involves giving space to acknowledge and label psychological experience. Living with an allergy can feel isolating and I frequently hear stories of people feeling dismissed due to their allergy not being taken seriously by others, which perpetuates feelings of isolation and self-blame. Therefore, it is vital that we acknowledge and validate the emotional experience associated with having an allergy, in order to help a person feel more confident in living with an allergy, normalise the experiences they are feeling and to provide empowerment. Furthermore, it increases awareness and helps to share the responsibility, because as in Ruth's case the lack of accountability of others resulted in her feeling at fault and further increased her feelings of isolation. I believe that we need to be pro-active and assertive in educating the world about allergies and the impact they have in a way which does not overwhelm people but which can build a strong network of support and allies around us. Allies who are maximising our protection rather than leaving us to face living with an allergy in isolation.

Once we have acknowledged emotional experience, we can then start to find ways of allowing these emotions space, in a way which strikes a balance between allowing them 'to be', whilst not holding us back from anything we want to do. Let's not forget that some anxiety, especially around situations which may hold some risk or danger, is not a bad thing and this is a completely adaptive way of our brain doing a good job of reminding us of the real dangers in the world; allergens included. However, we need good awareness of adaptive anxiety, because so often it can start to overspill into more hypothetical scenarios. Often after a traumatic reaction, it is common to find it more difficult to eat out, attend social gatherings and even eat foods that you were once comfortable with. Therefore, developing a plan that can support you to gradually, but effectively, get you back on track, is essential. Most of the time this cannot be achieved without the support of another person, hence the importance of talking about how you are feeling.

Ruth's chapter, 'The psychological impact of living with anaphylaxis' (Chapter 13) provides many other tips and strategies which can be helpful for managing anxiety, fear and anger and I would urge others experiencing similar to seek support and talk about their experience in the way that Ruth does."

CHAPTER 3

UNDERSTANDING THE SEVERITY OF ANAPHYLAXIS

Knowing that you have anaphylaxis is scary for you; and for family and friends it can be confusing. They may not know what it is and may feel reluctant to ask you, so the information in this book is to confirm and extend your knowledge, and for loved ones who would like to know more but are too nervous to ask.

Allergy is classified as a chronic disease by the World Health Organisation.

There are 14 major food allergens that are recognised in the UK (8 in the US) that have the potential to cause an anaphylactic reaction.

THE 14 MAJOR FOOD ALLERGENS ARE:

1. **Celery**
2. **Cereals containing gluten –** (including wheat such as spelt and Khorasan), rye, barley and oats
3. **Crustaceans – such as prawns, crabs and lobsters**
4. **Eggs**
5. **Fish**
6. **Lupin**
7. **Milk**
8. **Molluscs – such as mussels and oysters**
9. **Mustard**
10. **All tree nuts** which are almonds, hazelnuts, walnuts, brazil nuts, cashews, pecans, pistachios and macadamia nuts
11. **Peanuts**
12. **Sesame seeds**
13. **Soya beans**
14. **Sulphur dioxide and sulphites** (if they are at a concentration of more than ten parts per million)

Any food can cause anaphylaxis but the European Food Safety Authority and the UK Food Standards Agency have listed these 14 as being the foods most likely to cause serious allergic reactions and/or anaphylaxis.

People can also react with an anaphylactic shock to other allergens including:

- **Bee stings** and **wasp venom**
- **Latex**
- **Medicines** such as **penicillin, Aspirin, paracetamol** and **vaccines**[1]

Exercise Induced Anaphylaxis – there are rare cases where people can have anaphylaxis triggered by exercise. This can be caused by ingesting the allergen prior to exercise, most commonly from wheat, and can be avoided if the person does not eat wheat for at least 4 hours prior to any activity. However, it can also happen with no known trigger and can therefore be difficult to manage.

WHAT IS ANAPHYLAXIS?

An anaphylactic reaction, or anaphylactic shock, is an involuntary reaction in an allergic person's body. It is caused by an abnormal immune response to protein in a specific food or contact allergen such as a bee sting, or latex rubber. It can make the allergic person very ill and in rare cases, anaphylaxis can be fatal.

The body identifies the allergen as an invader, much like it does with a virus, bacteria or infection from a wound it needs to fight and heal. It goes into hyper-alert and starts to attack the allergen. The problem is that the allergen is not harmful, so the body then begins to overreact, causing the symptoms of anaphylaxis. Anaphylaxis causes your immune system to release a flood of chemicals that can cause you to go into shock – your blood pressure drops suddenly, and your airways narrow, blocking your breathing. Signs and symptoms include a rapid, weak pulse; a skin rash (hives); and nausea and vomiting.

It makes sense in some ways but in effect, the body is damaging itself and seems unable to stop the attack on the invading allergen. The body also has a very good memory, so it immediately identifies these allergens on subsequent exposures. This is the reason allergic reactions can worsen every time you come into contact with your trigger allergens.

It usually develops suddenly and gets worse very quickly. (For a full list of potential symptoms see Chapter 4.)

Anaphylactic reactions require immediate medical attention and an urgent call to 999 in the UK. Say: ANAPHYLAXIS when you get through to the operator. Adrenaline should be administered at this point.

In the worst cases, a person can die from an anaphylactic shock, but according to a study from scientists in the UK, Australia and US, this is rare and happens in only 1 per cent of cases. According to a study from Imperial College London, death by murder is more likely than death from anaphylaxis.

The chances are you will not know anyone who has lost a family member to murder or anyone who has been struck by lightning. These events, and anaphylaxis deaths, are very rare not least because we all go to great lengths to keep ourselves and our loved ones safe (details of the study can be found in Chapter 16).

This is good to know, but when you are having a reaction the 'feeling of impending doom' does not help you to feel confident about that. Watching your child have a reaction can be terrifying too; feeling completely helpless and not knowing what to do.

Other factors – There are other things that can affect the severity of allergic reactions such as exercise, stress, alcohol, menstruation and fatigue.

The TRACE Study, conducted by various universities including Cambridge University's School of Clinical Medicine and the paediatric department at Imperial College London, aimed to understand how exercise and sleep affected the outcome of exposure to an allergen. The objectives were to define the peanut reactive threshold in UK patients for the first time, and to define the effects of these two co-factors (stress and exercise) on the threshold and severity of reactions. The study found that exercise and sleep deprivation each significantly reduce the threshold of reactivity in people with peanut allergy, putting them at greater risk of a reaction if exposed to low levels of peanut. (Details of this study can be found in Chapter 16).

GETTING SOME PERSPECTIVE

It is important to remember that you are not anaphylactic. You do not have anaphylaxis all the time. This is how Frans Timmermans, the President and Chief Executive Officer (CEO) of the Dutch European Anaphylaxis Task Force, explained the condition to me at a European Academy of Allergy and Clinical Immunology (EAACI) convention many years ago. Frans felt strongly that people who are at risk of anaphylaxis should use the correct language in order to help them feel more in control.

'You are not your allergy!' A phrase which has been taken to the hearts of parents Tanya and Nadim Ednan-Laperouse, who in 2016, lost their 15-year-old daughter Natasha after she suffered an anaphylactic reaction to sesame seeds which had been baked into the dough of a Pret a Manger baguette. Following her inquest in 2018, the coroner expressed concern that the sandwich chain's: 'allergens were not labelled adequately or clearly on their packaging.' They campaigned for Natasha's Law which was passed in the UK and from October 2021 all food businesses that prepare, pre-pack and sell on the same premises have to include full ingredient labelling.

The Ednan-Laperouses now run The Natasha Allergy Research Foundation (NARF) in Natasha's memory, to help those with life-threatening allergies and to fund essential and pioneering allergy research with the goal of finding a cure.

> *"You do not 'have' anaphylaxis, you are merely at risk from anaphylaxis. You do live with restrictions, but your life is not restricted. It may feel like it is, but once you've got control back of your life and understand what is safe for you there should be nothing stopping you from enjoying a full life."*
>
> Frans Timmermans, President and CEO of the Dutch European Anaphylaxis Task Force

CHAPTER 4

HOW DO YOU KNOW IF YOU ARE HAVING AN ANAPHYLACTIC ATTACK?

Each person is different, and you may have one, many or all of the following symptoms. You need a diagnosis from a doctor to be sure they are caused by anaphylaxis, but if you do not already have a diagnosis, this should give you a good guide to understanding whether you are experiencing an anaphylactic reaction.

If you suffer with any of the symptoms on this list and you have not consulted a doctor, please do so as soon as possible. Symptoms can include the following:

- Itchy lips, mouth and tongue
- Coughing, breathing difficulties such as fast, shallow breathing
- Itchy skin, hives and/or rash spreading over the body
- Difficulty swallowing and swollen tongue
- Change in voice as airways constrict
- Wheezing and asthma attack
- Feeling dizzy and confused

- Feeling of impending doom
- Vomiting and nausea
- Swelling of the skin (angioedema)
- Stomach pain or cramps
- Feeling lightheaded or faint
- Increased heartbeat
- Clammy skin
- Confusion and anxiety
- Collapse or loss of consciousness

You can suffer different types of reactions to different allergens

It is interesting to note that the symptoms you get can be different depending on which allergen you come into contact with. They can also change over time.

It is important to remember that no two reactions are ever quite the same, so don't ever assume you know what is coming. Always be prepared; what starts off as a mild reaction can become a very serious anaphylactic attack on a subsequent exposure.

For instance, my own reactions differ from allergen to allergen.

Soya – An asthma attack, wheezing and tightening of the airways and sometimes hay fever like symptoms. It is interesting to note that whilst I cannot eat soya milk, flour or protein, I can eat the food additive soya lecithin, as there is no protein remaining.

Nuts – ground nuts/peanuts and tree nuts – If I eat peanuts or other nuts, I experience a kind of tingling or itching in my mouth and a strange feeling even in my teeth. It is hard to define, but as a child

I used to say my teeth felt claggy! I also experience swelling of the tongue and throat, and I shudder. This is hard to explain, but it is a sensation that starts from the throat swelling and makes my whole body, shake. I guess a sort of shivery feeling.

I often find I cannot speak or communicate easily due to the amount of swelling around my lips, tongue and throat. My throat becomes extremely painful, like someone is holding their hand around it and trying to suffocate me. My breathing worsens and asthma inhalers stop being effective. I also get hives all over my body which are insanely itchy. The feeling of impending doom is very frightening. You really do feel like something very, very bad is happening and that you might die. Probably because something very, very bad is happening! Your body is in fight mode and it is terrifying to experience.

Dairy – I start to feel the same claggy mouth/teeth feel. It is like I have itchy teeth and want to scrape them out of my mouth. Hives spread across my body, usually starting on my arms and chest. My body also becomes wracked with shaking, like some kind of seizure. I shiver and shake and become rigid with the effort of trying not to slip into more shock. My throat feels tight, my airways and lips swell and go blue and I cannot breathe. In the last few attacks I have also been unconscious pretty quickly so after that I do not know what is happening. I can remember snippets as if I am drifting in and out of consciousness. Sometimes I can hear doctors and nurses talking about me and I want to respond, to tell them the answer to their questions but, I cannot even move. It is a really weird sensation.

It is a frightening condition to witness and even more so to experience yourself. You may find that symptoms can change over time and worsen in some cases.

Sadly, fatal attacks happen when a person does not think that a particular food will cause such a severe reaction. A mild reaction can quickly become much worse, so always remain vigilant.

If in doubt, always administer your adrenaline and call the emergency services.

CHAPTER 5

GETTING A DIAGNOSIS

It can be very difficult to take the first steps towards getting a diagnosis for allergic reactions, but if you think you are experiencing any of the symptoms mentioned in the previous chapter there are a few things you can do that will help you to get a diagnosis swiftly.

See your doctor – Firstly, make an appointment with your GP to discuss your concerns, symptoms and what you think you are allergic to. If they feel you do have a serious allergy, they will be able to refer you to an allergy clinic. There can be very long waiting lists in the UK so be prepared to wait for anything from 3 to 6 months for your first appointment. Possibly longer... It is important to realise that your GP is a general practitioner and may not have an in-depth understanding of allergies. However, they should have enough knowledge to spot the signs of allergy and be able to refer you to a specialist.

Keep notes – Pinning down what is causing a reaction is sometimes difficult. It is a good idea to keep a food, mood and symptoms diary for a few weeks prior to your visit. Try to document what was happening during the time of your reactions. Detail everything and write down exactly what symptoms you experienced, where they appeared on your body and for how long. (See, 'Keeping a Reactions Diary' and the sample 'Food, Mood and Symptoms Diary' in Chapter 6.)

Take photos – Document what happens with photos of your symptoms e.g. hives and swelling. This will really help you explain things and help your doctor to understand what the possible causes and conditions are so that they can make a correct diagnosis of anaphylaxis if that is the case.

Do your research – Try not to google too much and get yourself worried but find out as much as you can. Talk to friends, find Facebook groups and explore. The more you know the easier it will be to get help. You will probably know someone who has this condition or knows someone who does. Speak to them and ask them how they managed to get a diagnosis. More details on where to find help can be found in the resources and references section in Chapter 16.

Finding a local allergy service – Unfortunately, there are far too few allergy clinics in the UK. (Check the resources section in Chapter 16 to find out if there is one located near you.) You may be able to get help through your local asthma or dermatology clinic.

Charities – Contact anaphylaxis and allergy charities including, The Anaphylaxis Campaign and Allergy UK. They will have people you can speak to on their helplines. They will certainly be able to listen to your symptoms and let you know if they think an allergy diagnosis could be the right outcome. They also have loads of information available to help you, including leaflets, handouts and support groups. You really need a doctor's referral to get a correct opinion and more importantly, help, support and advice about how to live with anaphylaxis.

Patient Advice and Liaison Service or PALS – If you think you are not getting the correct advice, support and information to help you with your allergies you can refer your case to PALS who should be able to help out. You will be able to find your local PALS service through your GP surgery, hospital or on the phone from NHS 111.

Clare Hussein, an allergy mum with a young daughter who has multiple allergies and eczema shared how hard it was for her to get that initial diagnosis. You can follow her on Twitter @Allergy_Mumof1, and on Instagram @south_coast_mum

She said:

> *It was a learning curve. I'd never experienced them myself, so we were starting from scratch. Initially I was on autopilot mode for practicalities and then when it sunk in, the magnitude of it hit and it was hard to get my head around.*
>
> *It was a very long road to diagnosis from the start of my daughter's allergy issues at six weeks old. Took until she was two years old to get a full allergy diagnosis, after plenty of GP appointments, reactions almost daily and no sleep!*

I struggled most with the worry that 'she will miss out on a normal childhood' initially. It upset me that she could not enjoy simple childhood pleasures like just going for an ice cream at the beach (this was before free-from ice cream was a thing). Getting people to understand why we needed to make the changes or ask the questions we do was also tough. Even as recent as eight years ago knowledge was scarce for most around severe allergies. I would urge parents to ask the questions and speak up even when it's the last thing you want to do, you are your child's best advocate.'"

CHAPTER 6

ACTION PLAN

SO, YOU HAVE A DIAGNOSIS – NOW WHAT?

This book is really designed to help you bridge that huge gap between floundering in symptoms, fears of the terrifying unknown, and then wondering how on earth you cope with this monstrous diagnosis. You now have a condition that could kill you, which is not something that is easy to come to terms with.

Dr Adam Fox, Professor of Paediatric Allergy, Guy's and St Thomas' Hospital, shared his advice on staying safe and avoiding severe reactions.

He said:

> *Fatal reactions to food are thankfully, incredibly rare. Despite a marked increase in recent years in the number of severe allergic reactions being treated in hospital, there does not appear to have been an increase in deaths from anaphylaxis.*

It is important to remember that anaphylaxis is uncommon in children with food allergy and that the overwhelming majority of anaphylaxis ends in a complete recovery. Frustratingly, severe reactions are unpredictable so although they are more common in people who have previously had one and in people with asthma, you can still have a severe reaction without these risk factors. Some things make severe reactions more likely – being a teenager, male, non-Caucasian, nut allergic (or milk allergic as a younger child) but there is nothing you can really do about these. In almost all of the very rare cases of fatal anaphylaxis, there are a number of contributing factors that lead to a bad outcome and it seems that it's only when a whole range of things go wrong, that the result is fatal.

Having now spent some time working as an expert witness, there are some consistent messages that come through the detailed analysis of individual cases that happen as part of the coroner's inquest. If you or your child have a food allergy, then many of these messages may sound very familiar to you, but I wanted to highlight some key areas to help you to always stay prepared and try to minimise the chance of you or your child having a severe reaction."

DR FOX RECOMMENDS SOME THINGS YOU CAN DO BEFORE A REACTION OCCURS:

THINGS YOU CAN DO BEFORE A REACTION:

1. **Make sure you or your child's asthma is well controlled** – Asthma is a major risk factor for severe allergic reactions (featuring in 70 per cent – 75 per cent of fatal food anaphylaxis in published UK and Australian studies). Poor asthma control, and the resulting

underlying airway inflammation, predisposes to the bronchospasm (tightening of the airways) which is characteristic of severe allergic reactions. Asthma is very common in children with food allergy but studies of previous cases of severe food anaphylaxis have shown that life-threatening bronchospasm was most likely in patients with severe asthma and less so in patients with milder asthma so making sure that if you or your child has asthma, that it is both correctly identified and adequately treated is very important. My personal practice is to treat asthma, in patients with food allergy, quite aggressively so as to ensure not only are they at a decreased risk of an asthma attack but also so that it is less likely that their asthma will contribute to a severe allergic reaction. Good asthma control means making sure that you have the correct medicine, that it is taken regularly and in the correct way (one of the most common reasons for poor asthma control is either not taking puffers or taking them incorrectly). It also means being aware that if asthma isn't well controlled, for example, you or your child need the blue puffer more often or are getting regular symptoms, then you need to raise this with your doctor. It you are worried, using a home peak flow meter or doing a regular Asthma Control Test, can help you keep a closer eye on things.

2. **Ensure you have access to two adrenaline auto injectors** (AAIs) at all times and that you know how to use them. The key step in the management of anaphylaxis is prompt administration of adrenaline and that is why people at risk are given Epipens, Jext or Emerade devices to carry with them. This requires education and understanding around the recognition of severe symptoms and how to respond to them. If you are not completely clear how to use the device (especially if you have had your device swapped

for a different one because of shortages), make sure you ask your GP or your practice for training and, in the meantime, look on the company website where you will find training videos and training devices. Request a trainer device so you and other carers can practice. In cases where one dose of adrenaline has been given, about 20 per cent – 25 per cent required a further dose, so it is really important to have two available at all times. In most cases, the second dose is given by a paramedic but having two, reduces the risk of there being a problem if the first device does not work properly (which is very rare).

3. **Ensure yours and your child's AAIs are the right dose and are in date** – AAIs come in different doses and have an expiry date on the side. They can still be used after this date, as long as the fluid in the window in the side is clear. You can register you and your child's device on the AAI company website so that you get a reminder in good time to get it renewed. As your child gets bigger, make sure that they have the right device – once they are over 30kg they should have a 300mcg device (although these are fine from 25kg), and from 12 years of age (unless they are particularly small) they should have a 500mcg device.

4. **Ensure you have a British Society for Allergy and Clinical Immunology (BSACI) Allergy Action Plan and that you understand it** – Every child and adult with food allergies should have an Action Plan for home and school and the ideal is that everybody uses the same template from the BSACI – these can be downloaded from bsaci.org/actionplans by your doctor so if you don't have one, ask them to complete one for you. It is important that you familiarise yourself with it and that school have done the

same. Go through scenarios in your head and make sure you are clear what you would do, especially if you are travelling overseas, to ensure you know how to call for help. The BSACI plans are very clear that you should use your AAI at the first sign of a severe reaction and another 5 minutes later if things haven't improved. They are also clear that if you are unsure if symptoms are severe enough, just use the AAI anyway. Delay in use of AAIs, despite the presence of severe symptoms is a common theme in fatal cases.

5. **Ensure school or work has your Action Plan and the AAIs** and that these are the right ones. Assume nothing and make sure that school and work has an up-to-date copy of the BSACI Allergy Action plan and that they have two AAIs and a clear process to ensure they are in date. Do not feel bad if you need to remind them that they are close to expiry! Schools can keep spare pens for any child where their pen can't be quickly accessed or didn't work, but this is a voluntary scheme, so encourage your school to be part of it (sparepensinschools.uk).

6. **Get an accurate diagnosis** – Make sure you know exactly what you or your child's allergies are. If you are unsure, pick this up immediately with your doctor.

7. **Understand food labelling** – The best way to avoid a severe reaction, is to successfully avoid the foods you or your child are allergic to. This is not always possible and mistakes or cross contamination will always be a risk but having a good understanding of food allergen labelling is key. Every adult and child with food allergy should have the chance to have this discussion with a registered dietician.

8. **Make sure you are understood** – When ordering food in a cafè, restaurant or take away, make sure you communicate your allergies clearly and to everyone you deal with. If you do not feel you have been understood or properly heard, then raise this with the manager. If you still do not feel understood, then it's best to avoid eating there. If you eat something and start to feel unwell, stop eating it. If you are going overseas, take translation cards (available from the allergy charities).

THINGS YOU SHOULD DO DURING A REACTION:

1. **Use AAIs at the first sign of a severe allergic reaction.** As soon as there is any suggestion that you or your child's breathing is involved for example, difficulty in breathing, wheezing, chest tightness, voice changing, throat closing. If things change with your blood circulation, for example, dizziness, light headedness, confusion – just get on and give the AAI. This means using it before calling 999 for help, before antihistamines, your Ventolin puffer or steroids.

2. **When in doubt, use the AAI.** Adrenaline is harmless so if you use it for a mild reaction, it won't do any harm. It's better to use it when you didn't need to, than to not use it when you did. If you are unsure if symptoms warrant adrenaline – give it anyway.

3. **If things are not clearly improving within 5 minutes of using the first AAI, use the second AAI. Do not delay.** If you aren't sure, give it.

4. **When calling 999, be clear to state that the problem is ANAPHYLAXIS.** Be clear that there is a life-threatening allergic reaction that needs an urgent response.

5. **Don't stand up.** Outcomes are better when the patient stays sitting or lying down with legs raised to help circulation and ensure a good blood supply to the heart.

6. **Avoid cofactors.** Do NOT exercise, do NOT get on a plane, do NOT drink alcohol if you have just had an allergic reaction – all of these can make it worse.

7. **Get help, even if you feel much better.** If you use an AAI, always call an ambulance or go to A&E as there is a small risk of a 'late phase' reaction up to 2–6 hours later.

> *"Remember, severe reactions are rare, but I believe that if you have these messages straight, then you can help to reduce the risk of bad things happening to you or your child."*

SOME OTHER THINGS YOU CAN DO TO HELP:

Dr Adam Fox talks above about getting an accurate diagnosis for allergies, the following advice may help.

Keeping a reactions diary

This is something that often gets overlooked. It can be hard to recall exactly what happened after the event, but it is vital that you do so if you are to track down the allergens you react to.

Remember to record the following:

- Exactly what you ate, and keep packaging if applicable.
- What time you consumed the food and how long it was before a reaction took place.

FOOD, MOOD AND SYMPTOMS DIARY

To help you identify problem and trigger foods and pinpoint which to eliminate

	Breakfast	Snacks and drinks	Lunch	Snacks and drinks	Tea	Supper	Supplements/ Activities	Mood and symptoms
MONDAY								
TUESDAY								
WEDNESDAY								
THURSDAY								
FRIDAY								
SATURDAY								
SUNDAY								

 Please seek medical advice from your doctor or specialist before cutting out any major food groups and if you think you have an allergy, intolerance or IBS please visit a dietician or nutritionist. For these records to be useful, please keep food packages so specialist can refer to ingredients lists.

- What your symptoms were, where they occurred in or on your body and how long they lasted.
- Take photographs of any visible reactions.
- How did you react? Did you take any medication? Did this help?
- Where were you? What were you doing, and who were you with?
- What else was going on. For example, were you stressed, tired, drinking alcohol, on medication, menstruating?

Do this as soon as you can so that you do not forget the detail. This is also useful for your child's reactions. You can then show this to your doctor or specialist, as details can become hazy in your memory if you have not made a note, especially after such extreme and distressing events.

I have created a food and mood symptoms diary (see previous page) that is also free to download from whatallergy.com/freeresources

Why write an Action Plan?

Dr Adam Fox talks earlier about always carrying an Action Plan. Research also shows that doing so reduces your risk of reactions.

Research into patients who carry an Action Plan show that those who do, have far fewer reactions. Why is this? They have spent more time assessing risks and putting plans into place, so are better able to avoid accidents happening in the first place.

'Preparedness promotes optimal outcomes'

The American Academy of Pediatrics also recommend drawing up an Action Plan. They said:

> *"Prompt action, administering adrenaline early and following the correct procedures helps to promote the optimal outcomes, for example, less severe reactions. That is what we all want so please be prepared. Write an Action Plan, keep it up to date, review it regularly and carry it with you always."*

Like any potential emergency, this is your risk assessment and you should review it after any reactions that do take place. Can you learn from the experience and amend your Action Plan?

You might be thinking you do not need an Action Plan; that you know what to do; that it is quite simple. But if you are in a stressful situation it can be almost impossible to remember even the simplest thing. You panic and start to behave in quite irrational ways. This is perfectly normal, and you should not worry about it too much.

It also means that anyone who is with you or your child, whether it is a friend, teacher, paramedic or a complete stranger who happens to be around, can consult it to help you in an emergency. It will be hugely helpful if you are too panicked or too ill to remember what to do yourself.

It is just one way to help you feel more in control; as is practising how to administer adrenaline, which we talk about in the next chapter.

MANAGING YOUR ACTION PLAN

As mentioned by Dr Adam Fox, you can visit the BSACI website to download Action Plans for children. These are PDF documents that you can print out and fill in. All you do is select the type or AAI you have; Jext, Emerade or EpiPen and download a copy. I would suggest doing this yourself as they do wear out, even if just folded up in your emergency kit.

Consider keeping it inside a clear plastic pouch to protect it as mine disintegrates regularly. Or maybe laminate a copy.

You can download a blank UK Action Plan from the British Society for Allergy and Clinical Immunology (BSACI) or one from **foodallergy.org**.

Or you can draw up your own using the information given here.

DESCRIBE YOUR SYMPTOMS – What your anaphylaxis looks like when you are having an attack, what symptoms you have? It may not be all the symptoms listed earlier in the book so explain what happens to you or your child in your plan.

Make sure you also save a copy on your computer so you can update it and print new copies if any get mislaid or wear out.

ANAPHYLAXIS ACTION PLAN

Name: ______________________________ Date of birth: ______________________________

Known allergy/allergies: ______________________________

Contact numbers: ______________________________

Next of kin name: ____________________ Telephone: ______________________________

GP Name: ____________________ GP Telephone: ______________________________

Medicalert Number: ____________________

SYMPTOMS DESCRIBED

What anaphylaxis looks like for me

Tingling, itching mouth, throat and tongue	Looking pale, grey and not right
Nettle rash, hives spreading on lower arms, chest, neck and face	Nausea
Swelling of tongue and face	Breathlessness and trouble breathing and speaking.
Feeling anxious and sensing impending doom	Uncontrollable all over body shaking
Increased anxiety	Passing out, unconscious

IMMEDIATE ACTION

Important – Do not walk, stand or move at all. Stay sitting or lying down, whatever is most comfortable for breathing but do not move.

- Call 999 (note the time you called). Do not leave the person alone. Send someone else to meet ambulance if you can. Stay on the phone.
- Administer adrenalin x 1 dose into thigh, midway and outside edge (Note time)
- Take antihistamine — 2 tablets
- Take inhaler – Blue salbutamol
- Monitor breathing and administer second adrenaline injector if deteriorating and no improvement within ten minutes. Always inject into the other thigh. (Note the time)
- Put in recovery position if unconscious.
- Dispose of used injectors safely

Sample of a UK allergy and anaphylaxis plan from the NHS

CHAPTER 7

TRAINING TO USE YOUR ADRENALINE INJECTOR

GETTING TRAINING

Once an adrenaline autoinjector has been prescribed, it is important that you and your family and friends know how to administer the drug in the event of an allergic reaction. As we discussed in the last chapter, your Action Plan is the first step. You know what to do. Now you need to make sure it is instilled into you so that you can take action in an emergency situation.

Adrenaline is always injected into the outside of your thigh and one important thing to note is that if you need to administer a second adrenaline autoinjector, you should inject the other leg. Do not administer both into the same thigh.

CARRYING YOUR ADRENALINE AUTOINJECTORS (AAI) AND KEEPING IT SAFE AND EASY TO FIND

The important thing here is that you should always carry two adrenaline autoinjectors with you, but what do you carry them in?

There are companies who provide cases that will hold just two pens, or larger cases that will hold antihistamine tablets, asthma inhalers and autoinjectors. It is a problem when you are going out, especially as men do not often carry a bag and women do not always want to carry a large bag. The medical paraphernalia is not insignificant but is nevertheless very necessary.

- Buy a simple, clear, Ziploc pouch. You can get these from most stationers very cheaply. It is the cheapest option and works well. I have done this for years.

- Buy a special bag to keep your medication together.

- Use something like a make-up bag. My autoinjectors, inhaler, antihistamines, emollients and pain killers are currently languishing lavishly in a Ted Baker clutch. The poshest AAI bag I have ever had!

EXPLAINING THE THREE AAIs

There are three adrenaline injectors on the market, and they are all slightly different.

I explain the main differences here and also outline how to administer each different AAI.

	Adrenaline dose, mg	Needle length, mm	Expiry/Shelf life in months
EpiPen Junior	0.15	13	20
EpiPen	0.3	16	20
Emerade Junior	0.15	16	18
Emerade Young Adult	0.3	23	18
Emerade Adult (60kg+)	0.5	23	18
Jext Junior	0.15	13	24
Jext Adult	0.3	15	24

EpiPen – www.epipen.co.uk

- Pull off blue safety release cap.
- Do not hold your thumb over the orange needle end on the right. People mistakenly inject their thumb so just hold it in your fist, as shown in the diagram above.
- Place orange needle end to outside mid-section of the thigh and push firmly into thigh. You should hear the needle click.
- Hold on your thigh for 3 seconds.
- Massage injection area.

Emerade – www.emerade-bausch.co.uk

- Remove needle shield.
- Press injector into outside mid-section of thigh and push firmly.
- Hold for 5 seconds.
- Massage injection area.

Jext – www.jext.co.uk

- Grasp the Jext injector in your dominant hand (the one you use to write with) with your thumb closest to the yellow cap.
- Pull off the yellow cap with your other hand.
- Place the black injector tip against your outer thigh, holding the injector at a right angle (approx 90°) to the thigh.
- Push the black tip firmly into your outer thigh until you hear a 'click' confirming the injection has started, then keep it pushed in. Hold the injector firmly in place against the thigh for 10 seconds (a slow count to 10) then remove. The black tip will extend automatically and hide the needle.
- Massage the injection area for 10 seconds. Seek immediate medical help.

In all three cases you should dispose of the needle in a safe place after use and always seek immediate medical help after administering any AAI.

These all appear easy to use, but in an emergency situation you may get confused or start to panic. Very sensible and normally calm people (including doctors) have managed to inject their own thumb instead of their, or their patient's thigh so make sure you familiarise yourself with how to administer all three types of pen, but most importantly your own.

If you need to administer adrenaline for someone else who carries a different type of injector, it is just as important to understand the subtle differences.

GET PROFESSIONAL TRAINING

When you are given your AAI, you should be shown how to administer it correctly and you should also be given a trainer pen – which is a replica injector with no needle so that you can practise injecting safely at home.

If you do not have one, you can get these free from your adrenaline injector manufacturer. Go to their website to request one. (See Chapter 16 for contact details.)

The Anaphylaxis Campaign provide Allergy Wise training for families and carers. It is an online, e-learning portal, so anyone can take advantage of this training at home.

The training is completely free, although you can pay for a certificate, especially for your child if you choose to. Getting a certificate for them will help them feel more confident and remind them that they do know what to do because they have done the training.

The more times you practise, the better you will get at using and demonstrating your injector to others. It is really important that you show everyone who needs to know, how to use your AAI.

Visit the Anaphylaxis Campaign website to find out more. (Link to course details in Chapter 16.)

SHOULD YOU ADMINISTER AN OUT OF DATE AAI?

If all you have available in an emergency situation is an out of date AAI, then you should use it. It will be better than not injecting any adrenaline at all.

Here's some information to put your mind at rest and explain how the drug degrades over time:

The US Food and Drug Administration agency (FDA) have extended the expiration date on EpiPens by 4 months.

> *"While both methods studied showed that the expired EpiPens contained less epinephrine compared to the non-expired EpiPens, there was still a surprisingly high amount of epinephrine in the expired EpiPens... Many EpiPens that were 2 to 3 years past their expiration date had more than 90% of the original dose remaining."*
> **verywellhealth.com**

The Food Allergy Research and Education's (FARE) medical advisors believe that properly stored epinephrine auto-injectors should be safe and effective to use up to nine months after the expiration date. Extending auto-injector use by nine months matches the FDA guidance on the extended use of pre-filled epinephrine syringes, which can be in short supply.

Australia do not advise using out of date injectors but say that it is safe to do so if that is all that is available.

PRACTISING WITH A TRAINER PEN

It is a good idea to do this regularly, especially with children, to help them become familiar with their AAI. Why not simulate an emergency where a favourite toy needs adrenaline and is having an allergic reaction?

Role play with your child, take them through each step of what they would do, and use the trainer pen so they can inject their toy to make them better.

PRACTISE INJECTING OLD EXPIRED PENS

I hope that all of your AAIs expire and that you never have to use one in an emergency. If you do find that you have old expired injectors, do not just dispose of them when you order your new ones. Invite a group of friends or family and practise injecting for real into an orange. This simulates a similar amount of required pressure as your thigh, and really does feel real when you hold a full AAI in your hand and prepare to inject, even if it is just into a piece of fruit.

You will need to be careful because this will mean using a real AAI with a needle. If you are doing this with children, an adult must be present. It can be dangerous, especially if adrenaline is injected into the wrong part of the body, your thumb for example, so take extra care that the child is fully aware of which end the needle is in and takes time to inject correctly.

To avoid injecting into the wrong area, hold the pen in your fist and never ever put your thumb over the top, in case you put it over the needle end by mistake.

If you, or anyone else, injects adrenaline by accident, call 999 and get checked out. There should be no real danger in an adrenaline dose being injected by mistake, but you should seek medical advice if it happens.

To recap: Follow the steps above on how to administer your particular AAI and simply have a go by injecting your poor orange.

NB: Please do not eat the oranges afterwards! Make sure you throw them in the bin after injecting them.

If you need to administer both adrenaline autoinjectors, always inject in your left and then your right thigh.

TIPS FOR GETTING THE MOST OUT OF YOUR AAI

It goes without saying that you should always carry your AAI at all times, but there are a few other things that you should always do to make sure you are always prepared.

1 Register online at your AAI supplier's website.
2 Set up expiry reminders in your diary.
3 You can also set up expiry reminders via the AAI websites.
4 Download your supplier's app for your mobile device, tablet or computer, and set it up.
5 Order a safe, hot and cold resistant carry case or find something you are proud to carry with you. If you carry a medical bracelet, a paramedic will know to check your bag for your medication.
6 Update your medical bracelet with all your allergies and mention you carry adrenaline.
7 Always carry two AAIs.
8 Print off your Action Plan and keep it with your AAI at all times.
9 Also carry the trainer pen so you can safely demonstrate your AAI.
10 Keep antihistamine tablets and an asthma inhaler in your emergency kit.
11 Always wear your medical bracelet in case of emergency.
12 Tell your friends and family where you keep your medication so they know what to look for should the need arise.

CHAPTER 8

SURVIVING THE DAY-TO-DAY

The only medications that can help in the event of an allergic reaction are antihistamine tablets, asthma inhalers and adrenaline.

I have been unfortunate to have had a lot of very severe reactions, mostly from eating out when food outlets have not understood my needs or have made a mistake. It is very upsetting when you know that your allergic reactions are all avoidable and happen because mistakes are made. Building up trust is hard when you feel that you cannot trust anyone.

Here are a few simple tips that I follow, which have now become second nature:

BE PREPARED

- Plan each day: work trips, school trips, parties and days out.

- Make sure that you know where you will be eating.

- Speak to them or take your own food. Take safe snacks too.

- Get to know what to buy each week on your shopping trips so that you have handbag safe free-from food to tide you over.

- Always carry your medication and wear a medical bracelet.

- Once your Action Plan is written, you will start to get daily routines organised so that all these things become habit.

Once you get used to your own routine, this kind of thinking becomes easier. I look at each week and work out what will be necessary for the following week. Sometimes I forget and mess up, but what helped me is to realise I will not starve to death if I miss a meal. Better to be safe than sorry. Don't beat yourself up or get cross or angry, just keep on learning; it gets easier. And there is always fruit and ready salted crisps! I try to have a stash in the boot of my car containing things like oat cakes, so that at least I am prepared when I am under my own steam.

ATTEND REGULAR CHECK-UPS

- **Make sure you attend your regular appointments at the allergy clinic.** Don't miss appointments as people wait a long time to get seen. It's important to stay on top of things, discuss your concerns and learn about any new advancements of treatments.

- **Visit your dermatologist** as well as your allergist if your skin is a concern. There may be things you can do: better emollients, treatments or regimes.

- **Keep regular appointments with the asthma clinic.** According to the organisation Anaphylaxis Campaign, having well controlled asthma is essential as poorly managed asthma could lead to a worse reaction. In June 2019, they released a statement, which says: 'Evidence suggests that poorly-controlled asthma will raise the chances of any allergic reaction being severe. If your asthma is troublesome and not well-controlled, and you have an allergic reaction to a food or substance, the reaction could be much more serious.

ALWAYS CHECK INGREDIENTS

- **Check, check and check again** – This is especially important when you are out shopping. I still miss things sometimes in ingredients lists, the writing can be tiny and hard to read. Do this in restaurants too, if you can. If they use anything packaged, check it and if you can't check it, don't eat it!

- **Never assume something is safe** – Do not assume the product recipe has not changed, even if you know this product is good, keep on checking because ingredients can, and do change.

- **The final check** – Get into the habit of just having one last scan before you open the packet to eat it. The number of times I have spotted an allergen at this point is enough to warrant me still being this paranoid.

- **Don't get complacent!** – The problem is that we want it to be okay, so we often read what we want to see, not what is actually there. Your checking skills may be rushed, and you could easily miss things. Recently I missed dairy, even though it was the largest and first ingredient in the list. It said 'Ingredients: **Buttermilk**, blah, blah, rest of ingredients listed.' I think because it was in bold next to the word ingredients, my brain just did not see it. When I checked after consuming a bite and my lips were beginning to itch and swell, of course I saw buttermilk listed quite plainly!

BE CAREFUL WHEN EATING OUT

Be doubly sure when someone else is preparing food for you that they understand your allergies. This is where most of my serious reactions have happened, when I've trusted the word of a waiter, chef or restaurant owner that their food is safe, and it most certainly has not been. Sometimes it is poor communication, lack of understanding or just sheer lack of care. If you have not seen a list of ingredients or feel 100 per cent certain that the staff are sincere and understand, trust your gut instinct and do not eat the food. (We have much more on this subject in Chapter 10.)

Use your eyes

If it looks dodgy, or is a readymade product such as bread, do not eat it. Not unless you check, check, and double check that it is genuinely safe. Dairy-free alternatives for instance can look exactly like the milk containing product, so never ever take that risk as they can be mixed up. Once a food is out of its packaging you can no longer really check. Insist on seeing ingredients.

Learn as much as you can

Do your research and make sure you know as much as you can about your allergies and how to stay safe. There are loads of great websites and some recommended reading and we have listed these in the resources section in Chapter 16.

Do be aware that there may also be many disreputable sources who just want to sell you their product. If anything says it will cure your allergies it is too good to be true.

Find like-minded friends and support

- **Contact people on social media** – There are loads of forums; Facebook, Twitter and Instagram communities that are brimming with topical and positive information.

- **Reach out to the allergy charities** – There are many in the UK, the two main ones being The Anaphylaxis Campaign and Allergy UK. If you do not have friends nearby who understand or also have similar allergies, these organisations may be able to connect you with people you can share, learn and meet up with. They often organise local allergy support groups, so find out what is going on in your area.

- **Build trust** – This is easier said than done, but by building some rapport and communication with people you will find they are more inclined to help, to go the extra mile and to really build up trust with you. It works both ways. People want to feel they can trust you and you need to be confident you can trust them.

- **Learn to love your life** – I have changed my life dramatically in order to stay safe. To reduce the stress and chances of mistakes, I favour entertainment that does not involve food, where I can. I love picnics and encourage others to indulge me in this. I get involved wherever food is concerned and help out at parties, take my own food, offer to bring free-from food and generally stick my nose in so that I am 100 per cent in control of this part of my life. It can be wearing but it can also save your life.

Teenager Thalina Houghton, who writes the *'allergies in bold'* blog, shared her views on coping with allergies at school and how grateful she is to the people who support her and how she has grown to appreciate things more since having multiple allergic reactions. A true reflection on a positive attitude to living with life-threatening allergies.

> *I'm extremely grateful that when it [anaphylaxis] happens in school I'm supported by brilliant teachers and friends. Anyone with severe allergies knows that sometimes it can feel isolating, like nobody understands what you must go through.*
>
> *By saying, 'please don't eat a certain food around me'. I am not being unreasonable because this is not a choice, it is not a diet choice. It is to simply save my life.*
>
> *My headteacher is very supportive and has gone above and beyond to make sure anyone at my school with allergies are safe. I have certain teachers to thank for truly saving my life and administering lifesaving actions when needed and although it wasn't one of my best days, it made me realise how humble I and everyone should be. What you have done for me will not be forgotten, Mrs Haynes especially.*
>
> *Turning my head to see my parents in resus made me realise that I'm not alone and never will be. Receiving messages from friends, who I have so much love for, gets me through the prolonged hours I spend in hospital.*
>
> *The world with allergies can be a scary place. Allergies can have*

the ability to interfere with everyday life whether that be attending school, going out for meals, or simply leaving the house but like any other condition, it shouldn't place boundaries.

I believe we all have something, for me, it's allergies. It may have affected a few aspects in my life but honestly, I have learnt so much about a condition that otherwise I'd know nothing about.

I use everything I experience living with anaphylaxis as a life lesson like viewing a situation from multiple angles and consider other reasoning besides my own.

Allergies – you have developed me as a person. I'm grateful."

CHAPTER 9

STAYING SAFE AT HOME AND WORK

PLANNING AND ORGANISATION

Coping with everyday life at home and at work is an ongoing task for anyone with life-threatening allergies. At home you can be in complete control, and with good organisation, have everything you need on hand, but even this can be an onerous task. In this chapter we look at how you can keep on top of planning and organisation in all elements of your life.

ALLERGIES IN THE HOME – SHOULD YOU BAN ALL ALLERGENS?

To have allergens or not to have allergens present? This is a big debate. I live alone so I can make sure I do not have any peanuts, dairy or other allergenic foods. However, I am quite happy to have normal milk in my fridge when I have visitors to stay. I also keep a stash of carefully labelled wheat-containing bread for guests in my freezer, as well as those tiny one cup milk pots you get in hotels (I collect them). This means I do not have to buy milk that will mostly not get used – I hate waste.

Storage – It is a good thing to have your allergens carefully stored, labelled and treated with the care and attention they need. Especially if other family members can eat peanuts and sesame seeds for example. Banning the whole family can create an unrealistic expectation of life on the outside, because your allergens will be present in most of the places you visit; for example shops, your workplace, friends' houses, restaurants, cafés and bars. You and your child need to learn to be vigilant in spotting dangers and identifying risks, so this can be a good learning activity.

Identification – Teaching your child what a peanut looks like, or how to check labels on a regular basis, will help them learn. Kids can be surprisingly responsible from quite a young age and will want to take some role in their daily care. Empowering them can be a useful lesson because they will have to do this for the rest of their lives. If you hide all the checking, planning and worry from them, they could struggle to cope themselves. There is obviously a fine balance and you don't want to transfer undue worry onto their young shoulders.

This is entirely up to you though and perhaps if very young children are the household members with the allergy, you may want to have a house ban on nuts for instance, while they are still little, just to be on the safe side. Once they are old enough to identify their allergen as dangerous and you trust everyone else in the household to keep to your high standards of care, bring the allergen back. Sometimes not having the allergen at all is the safest option.

This is just my opinion as I grew up in a house full of nuts; my Dad had a bit of a nut obsession and used to eat loads of peanut butter, and even make his own to save money. There were often bowls of nuts at family events and I survived. Although we once mistakenly put crisps into an empty bowl that had contained nuts. I would not advise this many nuts in the house of a nut allergic child, but if parents are responsible and eat them when the child is not around, it should be okay.

Nuts are probably the one allergen that I do ban, because eating them really is catastrophic for me. All my friends and family respect this and never eat them or have them out in the house when I visit. Milk, however, can be present and kept safe and away from those with the allergy. Despite my dairy allergy being very severe and possibly more dangerous than my nut allergy, I think it's easier to contain, to keep safe. Nuts and nut traces, are easier to spread and leave hidden traces.

It all depends how severe the allergy is and how you want to manage this.

SAFE STORAGE OF ALLERGENS

It goes without saying, all allergens must be stored carefully:

- Always use airtight containers, or seal allergens in Ziploc bags. Some allergens can leave more crumbs and residue than others: peanuts are dusty if salted, bread can leave crumbs everywhere, sesame seeds are completely uncontrollable!

- Make sure allergens are always carefully and obviously labelled and that you use stickers/labels that will not fall off, and permanent markers that will not wear off with time and handling.

- Store allergens on high shelves, out of the reach of children, where they cannot be picked up by mistake. Make sure the whole household is aware of the protocols in place and that everyone keeps the house safe.

- Always clear up spillages and crumbs immediately. Use soap and water, just running a cloth or sponge over them may mean either the surface, or cloth, remains contaminated.

STORING YOUR SAFE, FREE-FROM GOODIES

Treat your safe foods with the same reverence. For instance, when I was house sharing, my safe dairy-free fridge goods were all stored in one sealed and labelled container. This way I could be sure it was not contaminated, and not pilfered and eaten by someone else who did not need it. Many is the time my carefully rationed and planned free-from food had been eaten by someone else, only to leave me with nothing. It is not so easy to always replace free-from foods, so labelling can avoid unfortunate mishaps.

Also, keep cupboard goods in one container. Even in my own home I have one for crackers, crispbreads and oat cakes and a separate one for biscuits, snack bars and sweet snacks. It is good practise, especially when sharing with people who can eat anything they want.

COOKING AT HOME

This can seem utterly relentless. There is no break from it. It always feels like you need to be in control of preparing every meal because it is hard to trust others. Those of us with life-threatening allergies also tend to eat more meals at home because eating out takes so much planning and a huge dose of bravery and trust every time.

Here are a few hints and tips to help you get to grips with cooking at home:

- **Separate saucepans and baking tins** – If you are cooking for others with varying tastes and allergies, you can get used to doing this by having two separate pans on the go. One containing the allergen and one not. Make sure you do not mix up the spoons when stirring the contents and keep the lids on the pans so that the one with allergens cannot accidentally contaminate the one without allergens. (If the allergy is particularly severe you may not even have it in the house, but especially for intolerances, this can be a useful skill to master.)

- **Batch cook** – Buy some larger pans, get in loads of free-from ingredients and batch cook. Then you can freeze ready-made, safe, allergy-free meals that can be reheated quickly when you do not have the time or energy to cook.

- **Allergy cookbooks** – Invest in some good ones and experiment. It can get boring cooking the same old dull meals day in, day out. Get creative and explore. There are simply loads of safe foods out there, so have fun. Learn to cook some new dishes, and mealtimes will become far more fun and enjoyable. If you are not a natural cook, there are some simple cookbooks out there. Do some research and find one that works for you. Meals like simple pasta and stir fry do not take ages to cook. Roasting meat and veggies is fairly hands off and should not make you feel that cooking is always a chore. Here are a few tried and tested cookbooks. Be brave and explore. Many chefs now write their recipes with allergies in mind and will offer alternative ingredients which work just as well.

How to Cook for Food Allergies **by Lucinda Bruce-Gardyne**

One of the first cookbooks I bought contains loads of simple and easy to create recipes. It was also the book that taught me how to adapt other recipes to be safe.

The Wheat & Dairy Free Cookbook **by Terence Stamp and Elizabeth Buxton**

This one is probably my most loved cookbook. I used to buy Terence Stamp's wheat-free flour before other brands were around.

The Eczema Detox **by Karen Fischer**

This is a lovely cookbook and perfect for anyone who also has eczema in the mix. It is more than a cookbook and explores the different foods that can be good and bad for eczema skin.

Simply Italian, Simply Gluten Free **by Anna Del Conte and Michelle Berriedale-Johnson**

If you love Italian food, risottos and pastas this one is a must. I have taken three or four recipes as regular go-to meals. They are quick, simple to understand and divine!

Chocolate Treats **by Nina Modak**

Free from all the top 14 allergens – Nina has allergies herself and experimented in her own kitchen to come up with these brilliant recipes. If you have a sweet tooth, this one is for you.

Cooking Allergy-Free **by Jenna Short**

I own this one but have not really delved into it. The recipes look amazing and writing this has made me want to experiment more in my own kitchen, so I will be exploring this one more.

Deliciously Ella, Deliciously Ella Every Day and *Deliciously Ella, The plant-based cookbook* all by Ella Woodward – now Mills
She has written loads of cookbooks, mostly plant based. I do not own these, but her recipes look good. If you love cooking it could be one to investigate.

The Allergy-Free Family Cookbook by Fiona Heggie & Ellie Lux
It has good reviews on Amazon. For anyone cooking for a family it looks like a good one to try.

- **Google** – I must confess, I often get the iPad out, prop it up in the kitchen and search the internet for what I'm looking for. There are so many amazing bloggers out there sharing their own recipes you would be crazy not to do this too. Just use a bit of caution and check out your source before leaping in.

These appear on many free-from listings:

Eat Dairy Free by Alisa Fleming

The Kitchen Alchemists Cookbook by Frances Castelli

The Allergy-Free Pantry by Colette Martin (US book)

Allergy-Free and Easy Cooking by Cybele Pascal (US book)

The Gluten, Wheat & Dairy Free Cookbook by Antoinette Savill

- **Blogs and social media** – There are some brilliant free-from foodie blogs and social media pages full of useful recipes. Start to follow these, comment and share your successes and you will discover how helpful the free-from community can be. Here are just a few that you might find useful:

Allergies in Bold – Written by teenager Thalina Houghton who has multiple life-threatening allergies. For young adults check out **allergiesinbold.com**

May Contain – Written by Daniel Kelly who also has his own podcast, is great for young adults. He is a nut allergic twentysomething and a great role model for men with anaphylaxis, as we usually only hear from women. Check out **may-contain.com**

Glutarama – Rebecca Smith has a daughter who suffers with coeliac disease and she has food intolerances herself. She shares incredible baked goods recipes on her blog such as beetroot brownies and a self-saucing chocolate pudding! Her recipes are usually gluten and dairy-free and often vegan too. **glutarama.com**

The Intolerant Gourmand – written by Nathalie Newman who has a son with multiple allergies, this website is packed with hints, tips and advice for parents of allergic kids as well as blog posts and recipes. **intolerantgourmand.com**

What Allergy? – My own blog of course! Written by an adult with multiple allergies, eczema and asthma. Packed with inspiration, things I've learned and things that make my life easier. Embracing anaphylaxis and atopic dermatitis with a positive attitude. **whatallergy.com**

Allergy Insight – Written by health journalist Alex Gazzola, this blog is feisty. Alex talks about different issues facing the allergy community and is not afraid of a heated debate around a thorny subject. **allergy-insight.com**

Allergy Clinic London – Full of interesting and thought-provoking articles. Worth a follow for anyone with allergies. **allergycliniclondon.co.uk**

FreeFrom Farmhouse – Written by best-selling author of *Living with Allergies*, Emma Amoscato. Both her kids have allergies and her blog is a must read. She offers practical, no nonsense and sensible advice, giveaways and product reviews. **freefromfarmhouse.co.uk**

Michelle's Blog – Written by Michelle Berriedale-Johnson, the brains behind the FreeFrom Food and Skincare Awards. This blog is an eclectic mix of things that Michelle is passionate about, from allergies and electromagnetic sensitivity to global warming and pollution. It's a fun read and one to bookmark if you're interested in saving the planet! **michellesblog.co.uk**

The Legume Allergy Blog – Written by a mum to kids who are allergic to legumes and many foods outside the top 14. Packed with recipes, tips on living a legume-free diet and eating out with allergies. **legumeallergy.co.uk**

Eat Allergy Safe – Written by Nina Modak, an adult with multiple allergies. She talks about dating, anxiety, living with allergies and much more. **eatallergysafe.com**

Gluten Free Alchemist – This blog shares tips on travelling, recipes, life and parenting for coeliac children. If you are allergic to wheat, this is a great one to check out. **glutenfreealchemist.com**

Gluten Free Mrs D – Technically a coeliac blogger, this one has got in because 'Globetrekker' Sian shares tips on travelling whilst avoiding gluten, which can be very useful for those with allergies. **glutenfreemrsd.com**

Healthy House – This website looks at all the things you could be allergic to in your home, from bedding and dust mites, to electromagnetic frequencies. Well worth a read for anyone with atopic contact allergies. **healthy-house.co.uk**

- **Be adventurous** – Try new things! If you are allergic to nuts, there are thousands of fruits and vegetables out there that you can try. Don't let your food be boring, find new recipes and cook the food you love in different ways. I have recently discovered that spinach sweated in rapeseed oil and a clove of garlic is an absolute win. Suddenly, a calcium rich food like spinach that I used to find unappealing when it went all wet and soggy, became something I now love. It can take time to adjust but setting aside time to explore and try new things could bring you a newfound joy in food. Have some fun in the kitchen.

- **Focus on what you CAN eat** – I often hear people say: 'Everything has nuts in it or nut warnings,' which can seem to be the case, but it does not apply to meat, fish, fruit and vegetables. What I mean is, YOU CAN EAT EVERYTHING THAT YOU ARE NOT ALLERGIC TO! Even if you have multiple allergies, that is a lot of food. You may just need to cook more from fresh and avoid processed food with 'may contain' warnings.

- **Don't be scared of food** – When a particular food type has given you a serious allergic reaction, it can be easy to fear all food. It can make you lose all interest in food completely, especially after a bad reaction, as if your body now does not trust you to feed it. If you are feeling anxiety about eating, keep it simple at first. Start with basic foods you trust and slowly build up to include new things, but obviously, avoid your allergens at all cost!

SHOPPING – HOW TO AVOID ALLERGENS

This can be both a chore and an adventure. Life is hectic and we are all busy, so having to check every label can take ages and become very boring. It is a necessity for you though, and you must always remain vigilant.

- **Never assume a once safe product, is still safe** – Even if you think a particular product is safe, as you have eaten it before, always check because situations change. Recipes are updated or improved – you need to be aware of any missed allergens that may have been added. So always, always check, just to be safe.

- **Shopping online** – This can really help you as you can check all ingredients before buying and use the site's filter to avoid any searches that contain your allergens.

- **Reading, reading and re-reading labels** – Labelling is now so much better with all 14 of the top allergens requiring special attention; these will always be shown in **BOLD** under the ingredients section of the label. Often labels can be hard to read – especially if you are in a hurry and want to be able to eat something. We often read what we want to see and can easily miss an allergen.

- **Take your time and re-read multiple times** – I find it helps to read from the beginning. Then read backwards from the last ingredient. Do not skim-read and do not rely on the fact that allergens are always printed in bold. Even in bold, they are not always as easy to see, depending on the font, size of font and the background they are printed on. Black on white is far easier to read than white text on a coloured background. Food products are packaged to catch your eye firstly, not to communicate allergens. Legally, the allergens must be printed on the label but labelling allergens is not the first objective of the manufacturer.

- **Know your brands** – You will get to know what your favourite brands are and then your shopping can be done quite swiftly.

- **Keeping it fresh** – By this I mean, going back to the real basics. Sometimes this can make things so much easier, but you will need more time for food prep and cooking. I often just buy meat, fish, fruit and vegetables – no allergens there!

- **Go rogue** – Sounds weird right? But so many products are naturally free-from allergens or have had unnecessary allergens removed from the production process, every now and then it is a good idea to revisit sections of the supermarket that you think you cannot buy from. Read the ingredients labels on things you would love to be able to have and you may find some new hidden gems. I do not do this often, but when I have time to spare, I go on a supermarket voyage of discovery.

- **Watch the calories** – Some free-from goodies can be full of sugar, salt and fat to make them taste better and to ensure that the recipe stands up to mass production. For this reason, I see a lot of these foods as treats, just as I would for any biscuit, cake or packet of crisps.

- **Keep it clean** – I find that lots of processed free-from foods make me itchy and affect my gut. I am not allergic to processed foods per se, but I am sensitive to things that are not natural. You could try to avoid processed foods. Do you want to be eating loads of things you cannot even identify if the individual ingredients are separated out and put in a bowl? Does methyl cellulose sound appealing? Methyl cellulose is a chemical compound derived from cellulose, sold under a variety of trade names, and is used as a thickener and emulsifier in various food and cosmetic products. It is used to bulk out lots of gluten and wheat-free products. Other weird sounding ingredients like guar gum, extracted from guar beans; xanthan gum, made by fermenting sugar with bacteria, which is then solidified with alcohol, are emulsifiers and bulking agents and are commonly found in processed foods. Calcium propionate is the calcium salt from propionic acid and occurs naturally in butter and some types of cheese. It is a preservative found in bread and stops baked goods from going mouldy. I am not singling out these ingredients to demonise them – they have been designated safe for food consumption – I am just making the point that there are lots of manmade fillers, emulsifiers and flavour enhancers that do wonders for the look, taste and robustness of our free-from goods, but are they really good for us to be eating in large quantities? We just do not know. The old saying: 'If your granny wouldn't know what it was, don't eat it,' is a wise one. When you are coping with eczema as well as allergies, this tactic can really help.

- **I use a 5-ingredient rule** – I check for those things that do not sound natural. So, I can have things like oat cakes and a bottle of wine now and then. But I will never buy anything with a string of E numbers, additives, fillers and emulsifiers. Sometimes I do go wild and buy all the free-from, but I usually suffer some consequences afterwards. This is just my choice and it stops me missing hidden allergens as I am choosing simpler products from the shelves.

- **Bulk buying** – If you have space at home it can really help to buy free-from food in bulk. This helps avoid having to trawl the shelves too often. It can also avoid you having to go without as the supermarket shelves can often seem bare when your favourite snack has run out and there are no safe alternatives.

- **Request supermarket safe lists** – You can usually request a list from your supermarket of their safe products, filtered for your allergen(s). This can really help you save time and help you discover more things you can try. It can help you find the safe brands too, as things keep changing and new products come into the market all the time.

- **Check out the FreeFrom Awards** – If you are feeling lost and underwhelmed with the products you buy, make sure you are following the FreeFrom Food Awards run by free-from expert Michelle Berriedale-Johnson. Michelle runs the FoodsMatter website, writes a blog and is frequently asked by the press to comment on free-from issues. Every year, these awards in the UK champion the best of free-from food. I am continually discovering new products through the incredible work they do. There is also a FreeFrom skincare awards, which champions allergen-free skin products.

- **Attend Free-From Food Events, Awards and Shows** – There are lots of events you can attend, the most popular being The Allergy Show, which takes place in London, Birmingham and Glasgow every year. You will discover so many new products to try at these events, be able to question the manufacturers, try before you buy, hear from experts, and connect with others in the same position as yourself.

SURVIVING AT WORK

The same rules should apply here that cover staying safe at home and when you are out, but there are added complications that can make feeling included and valued at work extra tough. I have often felt very alone and excluded when work lunches and socials are arranged, and I cannot fully take part or do not feel safe. The important thing here is to be open and honest. Talk to people and tell them about your allergies. Tell people how you feel and what you need to do to stay safe, and most importantly, what needs to happen if you have an allergic reaction.

- **Tell your boss** – Hopefully work will be understanding and accommodating. I was really lucky in my last job to have a boss who went the extra mile. There would always be something suitable for me and being a very generous boss, the gifts she gave as a thank you, or for my birthday and Easter were always carefully checked for allergens and suitable for me. This hasn't always been the case. I have received so many dairy and nut containing Easter eggs at work in the past. They have always been gratefully received by my friends and family, so never go to waste.

- **Speak to your colleagues** – It is amazing how many of them will either have an allergy themselves or know someone who has. Knowing that they understand is really helpful. Having their support and help could be invaluable. Twice, I have had serious allergic reactions while out with my work colleagues, so they are now experts in my allergies. On both occasions they were so helpful, calling me an ambulance and going with me to A&E. I also found it helpful to have them discuss the incident with me afterwards. They had my back and were always checking things for me. I am still friends with and in contact with this lovely bunch. Thanks guys ;)

- **Also tell the human resources department** – Explain to them what your allergies are in detail. Make sure it is on your staff record that you carry adrenaline and where it can be found in the case of emergency. Give them a copy of your Action Plan to keep on file. You may also need more understanding and support, and this will be easier to get approved and arranged if you've been upfront at the start of your employment. If you're struggling, don't suffer in silence. It also means any company wide schemes will have you in mind when they otherwise might not.

- **Tell the office first aiders** – Find out who your office first aid volunteers are and introduce yourself. Offer to demonstrate how to use an adrenaline autoinjector if they do not already know. This should be covered in their first aid training, but a refresher is always welcome. They will also value being able to quiz you more than they might during training and will want to make sure they know what to look out for if you were to eat an allergen by mistake.

- **Demonstrate your injector** – I asked if I could show everyone in the company how to administer adrenaline and it was a really fun session that everyone got involved with. They all had a go using the trainer pens to pretend injecting each other and asked lots of questions. We also used some out of date AAIs to inject into an orange. It made me feel stronger and safer knowing that they all knew what to do in an emergency.

- **Tell everyone!** – You want everyone to be on the lookout for potential dangers because there will be times when you are not as vigilant. Having an army of colleagues aware of what could make you ill has got to be a good thing.

BEING EXTRA PREPARED AT WORK

There are also loads of other tactics and planning that I have used at every job.

- **The snack drawer** – Ever the girl guide, my snack drawer at work was a constant source of envy. It was always packed full of allergen-free crackers in their own container, biscuits, tinned soup, tissues, pain killers, spare inhalers... but mostly food! Keep it stocked for when you have brought in no lunch; when everyone goes to the ice cream van; when someone brings in doughnuts or cake that you cannot eat. You will have something to eat and not feel so left out. I try never to feel left out; it is not anyone's fault.

- **Bring in safe lunch** – It is a time saver for most people but for someone with life-threatening allergies, it can make life so much easier. Get into the habit of cooking more than you need and bringing in leftovers for lunch. If there is a microwave, you can heat up your food and cook jacket potatoes or other allergen free food. You will probably find your food is far healthier than your colleagues.

- **Tea and coffee** – It is that trust again. What goes on in the kitchen when your back is turned? I have watched so many people remove the teabag from my drink with the teaspoon they have just used to stir and retrieve the bags from their milky beverages. It is something we do every day of our lives, on autopilot, and it becomes habit. Some people will be careful, but some will not be, and it is not their fault, it is just how we are programmed. I rarely trust people to make me a drink. Not until they have been fully vetted and had the rules of 'making safe tea for Ruth' explained in full. These are as follows: Herbal tea, no milk, no sugar, leave the bag in. Make it first and set it aside to avoid cross-contamination. Same with coffee. No milk, no sugar. Do not stir. Do not touch once coffee poured. Put to the side so no milk gets into it by mistake. My favoured method of getting hot drinks at work though is always to take control and make them myself. Not only does it get me away from my desk for 5 minutes to stretch my legs, but then I KNOW my drink is safe. You will be popular too because everyone loves having a cuppa made for them.

- **Café, coffee shop runs** – Just be extra careful if you put in an order that a colleague is fetching from a nearby coffee shop. NEVER EVER take a sip through that plastic lid without checking you have the right drink. If you can, and have time, offer to help. They will be glad of an extra pair of hands and you can check that the café do not stir or contaminate your drink either. Unless you are going to be there when it is made at the café and can check, it is wise to avoid ordering a soya or other plant milk tea/coffee, as I have seen and heard of many cafés that either misheard or forgot and made the drink with normal milk. For example, oat milk can sound a lot like hot milk! It is just not worth the risk. Order it black and stay safe!

- **Vending machines** – These are a potential allergen risk. When the tubes are lined up next to each other, one dispensing the milk, the other hot water... can you guarantee the milk tube has completely stopped dripping for your black tea/coffee? No, is the answer. With this in mind I always make sure I am aware which facilities are available before accepting hot drinks and I always check if it is from a vending machine. My heart sinks when I see those monstrous vending machines. All I want is some instant drink (not my favourite, but safe) or a flask... Better to be safe than sorry so do not assume you know what you are getting. Always ask for clarification. It can be safer to stick with herbal tea or just ask for a glass of water.

- **Meetings** – You will not die of thirst or starvation for missing out on the meeting biscuits, but if you are a biscuit fan like me, make sure you have a pack in your desk drawer and sneak some in for yourself when you go to meetings, particularly long ones with biscuits provided for everyone else. If you are feeling particularly virtuous, take fruit instead. But biscuits generally help you get through most meetings better than fruit can. Except figs! Nothing tops figs.

- **Visiting clients** – Same rule applies. If you can, take lunch and snacks. If there is a meal involved, ask if you can have the name of the establishment so you can phone ahead and make sure it will be safe for you. If you find you have not had time to do this and are being invited to lunch when no pre-prep or checking is possible, be open and honest. Tell your host so that they know what you will need to do and that you will be checking. Go straight up to staff and explain that you would normally phone ahead and check to let them know. Explain your allergies and ask what they suggest is safe. Give them options of what you enjoy eating and most chefs will be very helpful. No one wants any customer to go hungry or not to enjoy their meal. I can eat eggs, so often end up with ham, egg and chips. Or I order a simple steak, or a salad with the dressing on the side.

- **Conferences** – These tend to be easier these days as most large hotel complexes are fully aware of allergens, and catering requirements regarding allergens. Find out who the main contact is and speak to them to find out what your options are for breakfast, lunch, and the evening meal if applicable. Make sure that you plan beforehand. Check a week before and go in early to introduce yourself. The easier you make it for the hotel the easier it will be for you. You will also feel calmer. It is also a good idea to take emergency rations. Rice and lentil packs that can be kept in the cupboard and are already cooked are a life saver for me. It is always better to be over prepared than to go hungry. Ask if you can book a room with a fridge so that you have somewhere to store your plant milk and other allergen-free goods. If this is not possible, ask if they can store your food in their kitchen fridge. Provide food in a well-labelled container, with your room number and name on it, to help keep it safe and easy to locate.

- **Surviving birthdays** – This is always a worry with the potential for feeling left out. The tradition in the workplace is often to bring in cake or to buy someone a cake on their birthday. Not so easy for the allergic person. I usually bring in my own, knowing that it is safe. I have had some really kind colleagues make me safe cookies and cakes. The kindness of others is lovely when it happens. Always ask colleagues to go through all the ingredients with you and take extra care when sampling these home-made cakes and biscuits. Have a tiny nibble first and wait and see if you have a reaction. Do not dive in heedless to the risks, and if you are at all unsure, just do not eat them. It is so hard trusting others, but you need to feel safe. Only when you are 100 per cent confident it is okay, should you tuck in with gusto. I would rather be alive and a little bit hungry!

- **Endless food** – Some offices can be full of biscuits, doughnuts and cakes on a regular basis. These are meant as a treat and to boost staff morale but if you are allergic to them, you can rarely take advantage. It helps to have your own food ready so you do not feel quite so jealous, but it can make you feel isolated, different and left out. See how unhealthy all this extra food is. You do not really need it, so can feel smug and healthy while others tuck in. Or why not ask for fruit to be supplied for everyone instead.

- **Social events and outings** – I do often miss out on these and I can honestly say for me, I am happy to miss out on most occasions. The anxiety I am dealing with means I must feel comfortable with what is proposed. If I am not, I will not go. Also, I do not want everything to revolve around me. I am not too bothered if the office has an outing to an Indian takeaway or a waffle bar. I am getting old anyway and more than happy with an early night. However, on some occasions, I feel it is okay to ask if I choose the venue. My colleagues are usually fine with this and we have had many a work lunch or meal out at Nando's, a local café or nearby steak restaurant. Be honest with colleagues. You can always go along just for a drink, something I have done a few times to be sociable when I have not felt brave enough, or the restaurant has not been suitable or safe for me.

- **The allergen infested workplace kitchen** – Most kitchens in the workplace will have milk and lots of potential for wheat crumbs. Depending on what you are allergic to will dictate how easy it is to avoid your allergen at work. I just got used to doing my own thing and did not mind cleaning up the mess in the kitchen before making my own lunch or drink. There was often milk spilt, so I would just clean it up. You just get on with it. If you are very allergic, speak to colleagues and ask them not to leave nuts around and to take care when eating the food you are allergic to. I did speak to one colleague who used to shell nuts and leave the shells and crumbs around on desks and floor and once my own desk. After talking, he was much more careful and stopped eating nuts at all when I was in the office. It is the same anywhere, keep a lookout for potential allergens. I also used to label my safe plant milk and dairy-free spread although most people steered clear of these, assuming they were unpalatable.

- **Dealing with mistakes** – I really struggle to trust people. I always try to explain how scared I am and just ask them to be mindful and honest. If they do not know or cannot remember the ingredients, they should never, ever guess. In my last job, although they did try hard to include me and cater for me, mistakes were made. I was given a 'safe' salad one day only to find feta cheese nestling under the iceberg lettuce. It just becomes safer and easier to provide your own food.

- **Dealing with feeling left out at work** – It is very easy to feel different and left out at work. I do feel that I missed out on some things just because I was a bit of a difficult person to include; always having to speak to the caterers so I could have a special meal. A free-from meal probably costs more too. In-office catering is just so easy when it is a lovely beige spread of sandwiches and food to pick from. It is my ultimate nightmare because there is often nothing suitable for me. The Christmas hampers and gifts, the Easter egg everyone gets given, and birthday cakes, are never suitable for someone with allergies. I used to try to include others in anything I brought into the office and to share homemade cookies and flapjacks for instance. Leading by example did make most people realise that what they brought in was not okay for me. It did not always make people change, but many of them did start to include me more. But then you have the fear of trusting that they have understood. You need to develop a thick skin and learn that this is what you must do to stay safe. Yes, you miss out on some office food, but you get to continue living this amazing life.

- **Dealing with the bullies** - I have been bullied at work and it is sometimes focused on my allergies. One colleague took pleasure in making fun of my 'free-from' food, implying it was somehow below par and she would never eat it. She once looked at my gluten-free toast and commented, *"That looks rancid!"* I cannot quite believe it when someone says something like that. It can be hard to take. I would usually ignore her or reply with something like this: "Good because there is none left to share with you!" You must think positive. If you are happy with your lunch, then that is all that matters. There will be people like this everywhere but thankfully few and far between. On a serious note, bullying is not acceptable in the workplace and if talking to the individual in question does not help, you should escalate matters and get advice. Your boss or human resources department should help you deal with any workplace bullying. (See bullying references in Chapter 16 for resources to help if you think you are being bullied.)

- **Dealing with thoughtless comments** – I have had all these comments over the years...

"What on earth can you eat? Dust?"

– Well, no, I'm actually allergic to dust too!

"Chocolate with no milk in? Must taste like cardboard."

– It is actually far healthier, has fewer calories and is very tasty. But do not worry, I am not offering you any anyway.

"Poor you, you can't eat any of this."

– Said as they fill their plate and tuck in!

"What has it got in it? Fresh air?"

– Or just general negative comments about anything free-from, vegan or gluten free.

Most people do not mean to be unkind when they say flippant things. They genuinely are amazed at how you cope. If they do upset you, explain with all the calm you can muster, that you do not appreciate their comments. Then educate them on how good your food does taste. You could say something like,

> *"I have allergies so can't eat normal chocolate, but this is safe for me and I really enjoy it. When you make fun of my food it makes me feel really awkward. Why don't you try some? It's actually quite nice."*

By being open and non-combative, I have normally managed to turn a negative person into someone who fights my corner. This does not always happen though. Just steer clear of toxic or judgemental colleagues.

The risk from bullies is potentially having your allergen sneaked into your food, which I hope would never happen. There are cases of this happening in schools but no data for the workplace. The lasting effects of bullying are higher levels of anxiety and poorer quality of work and home life.

- **Bullying for children with allergies is a real problem for many.** According to a US survey in the journal *Annals of Allergy, Asthma and Immunology*, about 25 per cent of children are bullied, teased or harassed because of a food allergy. When children under 5 years old were excluded from the results, the figure rose to 35 per cent, and among students in grades 6 through to 10, it was as high as 50 per cent. This is an uncomfortable statistic.

Daniel Kelly, founder, blogger and podcast host of may-contain.com has had an allergy to all nuts since he was a young kid. Now a young adult in his first job with an allergy blog, with his podcast as his hobby, he is passionate and vocal about the need to talk about allergies.

> *The best piece of advice I can give to young people is always to be vocal about your allergy when you're eating out with friends, or sharing a kitchen with new people. Always educate people about the seriousness of your allergy and never feel embarrassed to speak up about it. I have always found people are usually very understanding about an allergy when you tell them, and usually intrigued to find out more.*

I want to keep breaking the stigma around allergies and giving young people a voice. I want to make more young people feel more confident and empowered to speak up about their food allergy.

Over 25 people a year die because of anaphylaxis; if one less person dies unnecessarily as a result of May-Contain, then I will have achieved my goal.

A huge issue, which I'm trying to tackle, is that the ages 16 years to 25 years are most at risk of having an anaphylactic shock. It might be the first time they are moving away from home and they are taking on the responsibilities of managing their allergies.

I have always felt confident to speak up about my allergy and make others aware. However, this is not the case for most young people. I hope, in time, and through speaking up about this, more young people can feel more empowered to speak up and in turn, keep themselves safe."

CHAPTER 10

EATING OUT AND HOLIDAYS

These are the two most scary areas of my life. I cannot hide at home and must put some trust in others. When that trust has been betrayed many times, it is not easy.

Eating out has been the source of all my major allergic reactions, so I understand that you may be very scared about eating out. With careful planning, you should discover some local places where they are more than happy to include you and accommodate your allergies.

There is also: *'Never a holiday from your allergies'*. You must always be vigilant. It is hard, because both eating out, and holidays, should be experiences that mean rest, relaxation and indulgence. For the allergic person, it just means more of the same planning, preparation, worry and constant checking. Hopefully this chapter will help you find some enjoyment from both, with a little extra prep beforehand and the planning of a military operation.

EATING OUT

From October 2021, Natasha's law comes into force and requires all pre-packed food to display full ingredient and allergen labelling to all food prepared and packed on the same premises from which it is sold.

This should make eating out with allergies much easier and things continue to improve. Here are a few tips to help you to stay safe when you are eating out.

- **Phone beforehand to discuss your allergies** – Explain in detail exactly what you are allergic to. If you can speak to the chef in person that is most helpful. I find it helps to email the restaurant so that they have your specific requirements in writing, then to phone and chat it through to ensure they understand.

- **Tell them what you CAN eat!** Telling a restaurant what you like to eat can also be helpful. By telling them what you like you will get a meal you are more likely to enjoy. I often find that the chef prefers to prepare something completely different that is not on the menu. I guess that this is so that everyone knows it is for me and it does not go to the wrong diner – which has happened before.

- **Visit beforehand** – Phoning or emailing is great, but I find that visiting the restaurant before you go can be helpful. It means you can meet the staff and become a real person to them. You can check they have your allergen-free booking in the diary and if you are lucky you will get to chat to the chef, and they can go through the menu in person. This will really help you to feel safe.

- **Go early, when it is quiet** – Book the earliest available sitting so that the kitchen is clean, and you are one of the first served. Avoid booking during busy service times. The staff will generally appreciate this when you explain why you have done it because it can also be stressful for them ensuring an allergic diner is safe.

- **Places to avoid** – An investigation by the BBC's Panorama team found that takeaways are not the safest places to eat. The catering website Saffron found that two-thirds of takeaways are still breaking the law when it comes to allergens. Be cautious if you want to eat at Indian or Chinese restaurants and fast food takeaway outlets. Also avoid anywhere that sells street food where you cannot check the ingredients. It is just not worth the risk. Street vendors have probably not had enough training and may not fully understand the severity or implications of cross-contamination.

- **The Coeliac Society** – Coeliac UK provide gluten-free catering accreditation, which provides in-depth training on how to cater for someone who must avoid gluten in their diet. If your allergy is to wheat, this charity is really helpful. I find they are also able to avoid other allergens because they already understand fully the principles of safe handling and avoidance of cross-contamination in the kitchen. You can find links to their website in the resources section at the end of this book.. **coeliac.org.uk**

- **TripAdvisor** – Can be a great place to check for good reviews online when you are looking for somewhere in a particular town or city. **tripadvisor.co.uk; tripadvisor.com**

- **Blogs** – Google the restaurant you're interested in and you may find loads of bloggers sharing their experiences and advice.

- **Apps** – There are loads of new eating out with allergy apps springing up so it's hard to see which will work out and stay current. Two that are current at time of writing include *Glass Onion* and *Dine Pilot.*

HOLIDAYS

It can be scary visiting another country when you suffer with food allergies, but many people do successfully travel and enjoy local food. There are many things you can do to ensure you remain safe. It is about trust, again when it comes to eating out. A language barrier makes it hard to communicate and unless you are fluent, can you be sure the restaurant understands? Make sure you are as prepared as you can be when understanding the translations of your allergens in each country you visit. The charities Anaphylaxis Campaign and Allergy UK, provide translation cards in 35 languages. A set of 3 cards per language are available and they feature an alert message, an emergency message and a message for use in restaurants to ensure that your food is free of the allergens you are sensitive to. They cost around £15 per set. There are also language translation apps you can download, and of course, there is always Google Translate.

If you suffer one allergy, it is easier than if you have multiple allergies.

The safest and easiest options are those that give you control, so things like camping and self-catering.

Self-Catering

- Check whether there is a fridge and freezer.

- Take your own toaster so that you can be sure there is no cross-contamination.

- Take your own utensils and pans if you are really concerned. I know people who do this, but I think if you are happy to give things a quick clean when you arrive, most places I stay in are pretty clean.

- Batch cook and take most of your food with you so all you need to do is reheat.

- Book a supermarket delivery to arrive just after you do.

- Check out local farm shops – always a source of delicious and often allergen safe food that's also a bit more indulgent – you're on holiday, so treat yourself.

- Have a rota for cooking and carefully vet everyone so you do not feel you have to cook all your food for your whole stay.

- Take everything you need. This way you ensure you have all your favourite food, so you do not miss out. It's a holiday, so splash out on things that will help save you time but are still healthy and tasty. This is the time to buy pre-cut veg, just for holidays, so you can just bung it on rather than spending time chopping and prepping.

Festivals and Camping

This kind of holiday allows you to maintain a lot of control. You have time to carefully plan a break at a festival that involves camping, or if you are just going camping, you can check out the local area before for potential eating out and shopping opportunities.

Beware, at day festivals, they may confiscate any food that you try to bring in. If you contact them ahead of time, you can get special permission to take in your own food, especially if you have already spoken to them about the food choices available and can demonstrate that they are not suitable for you.

I always try to get hold of a list of the vendors for an event and contact them ahead of time. Usually, they are not suitable, but occasionally you'll get lucky. Being prepared and knowing that you need to take your own picnic and supplies helps you stay in control and hopefully there might be somewhere that is safe to eat!

I usually take lots of safe food that I can store at room temperature or rather, tent temperature.

- **Fruit** – I take lots of apples, blueberries and dried fruit.
- **Crisps, oat cakes, flapjacks** and other sweet and savoury snacks.
- **Non-meat items** such as vegetable bites, falafel, vegetables like carrots, courgettes and cucumber that are easily cut up and are not unsafe, or could potentially give you food poisoning when kept out of a fridge for too long.
- **Tuna** in pouches or tinned food that you can eat from cold.
- **Hard-boiled eggs.**
- **You can take tins of anything** but make sure you have a tin opener.

- **Better still, take a stove** to heat your food up.
- **I avoid taking any meat that is unsafe** without a fridge for storage.
- **Pre-cooked rice, quinoa and lentil pouches** that can be eaten cold.
- **Tea bags** and coffee.
- **Small, 250 ml plant milk cartons.** I have seen these for soya milk and KoKo coconut milk available in some large supermarkets and health food shops. One carton is enough for my morning coffee, breakfast milk and a swig to finish it off, so there is no milk going off in the tent during the day.
- **Also, take lots of sandwich bags and plastic boxes** to store food in. This means I can make up a lunch box to take with me, so I do not have to traipse back to my tent every time I need food.

Medical supplies

Make sure to complete a prescription renewal and that all items are in date:

- **Adrenaline auto-injectors** – Also make sure you carry a letter from your doctor explaining that you carry this due to a diagnosed allergy if you are flying.
- **Inhalers** – If you have asthma, always take a few and make sure they are full.
- **Antihistamines** – I take a combination of liquid bottled antihistamine and tablet form.
- **Emollient** – Decant into travel sizes.
- **Sensitive skin safe sunscreen** – If applicable. There are a few on the market suitable for people with eczema but many can irritate the skin, you do not want to get caught out without suitable protection. I use Green People SPF30 but also use SPF60 which you apply before dressing and let dry. It does not irritate my skin and gives good overall protection. I also use my normal daily sun

cream on top of the SPF60 if it is really hot.

- **Pain killers** – In case you do have an allergic reaction.
- **Bandages and dressings** – To help you cover any skin reactions to help prevent you itching them too much.
- **Cooling pads** – And my trusty travel portable fan to cool you down if your face becomes inflamed or affected by allergic reactions.

Do your research

Find out as much as you can about the place you are visiting before you go. You can find out when you arrive, but doing it in advance saves an awful lot of time. You can hit the ground running and not waste time faffing around on your holiday.

- **Learn the 3-digit emergency number** for the country so that you can call an ambulance if you need to.
- **Where is the nearest A&E hospital?**
- **Where are the local pharmacies?** Check late night opening times?
- **Find local farm shops and health food stores.**
- **Google local allergy friendly cafés, pubs and restaurants.**
- **Post on your social media** to see if friends and family have recommendations, or even whether you can hook up with an Insta buddy while you are away. I've found loads of Facebook groups in various countries and been able to get first-hand advice from people in the country.
- **Google 'allergy friendly holiday'**, and the place name you're visiting and look for cafés, pubs, restaurants that might be useful to investigate. Look out for bloggers who share their success stories.
- **Research the local cuisine** – If you're travelling abroad make sure you know what traditional dishes contain your allergen, and also the types of food you might expect.

Advice on flying with allergies

Being in an aeroplane with allergies can be a risky place to be so here are a few tips.

- Many airlines do not serve nuts on the flight but make sure you check and notify the airline when you book. Check again when you board the plane and ask them to do an announcement requesting passengers not to eat any nuts; they may have brought some on board with them.
- Take a packed lunch on long haul flights and safe snacks on any flight. Safe meals are not easy to order and may not be available. You can often order with one allergen in mind but not multiple.
- Make sure you always have your AAIs and medication with you.
- Take antiseptic wipes with you to clean down the seat and table if you are concerned about cross-contamination from the previous flight.
- Take a face mask in case you feel anxious or in case anyone else eats nuts or other allergens close by you; you should not have an airborne reaction but some people might so this might help ease any anxiety.
- Ask to be moved if someone does eat nuts and refuses to stop doing so. I've found most people understand and will put them away if you ask them politely.

CHAPTER 11

DATING

Dating with life-threatening allergies is daunting. You want to show your best self on a date, but need to be just as picky, fussy and neurotic as normal. You wonder: will anyone ever be interested in someone with such a limited lifestyle?

Hopefully, you will find that most people are understanding and accepting of your condition, just as if you had any other disability. If they are not willing to take it seriously and don't seem interested, they probably aren't the right one for you. If they ask questions and want to understand, that's a good sign at the start.

- **When do you divulge your allergies?** – When exactly do you drop the 'A bomb' as I like to refer to it? It is usually best to be upfront and discuss it on the first date, especially if you really like them. If you don't think you'll see them again then you can probably avoid the topic. I also mention it in any online dating biography because if it puts them off, it is not worth engaging in conversation. I have seen advice that you should hold this information back, because it is about you as a person and not your limitations but so many people disappear, ghost you or go quiet when you get to discussing it that I just feel it saves a lot of time-wasting to get it out there.

- **Wear your medical jewellery** – If you wear a medical bracelet, the observant date may ask about it. Most people are aware why these are worn – to alert paramedics to a medical condition. This is a great opener to explaining your allergies.

- **Be confident and succinct** – Just tell them you have a life-threatening allergy, explain what you are allergic to, that you must carry adrenaline and even a tiny trace of your allergy could cause an anaphylactic reaction. You have nothing to be ashamed of and anyone who cannot handle this will let you know. They usually just disappear. Great for weeding out the time wasters.

- **Taking control of the situation** – You can choose a destination for the date that you know is safe for you and if you decide to go out for a meal, make sure you offer to book it so that you can phone and/or visit beforehand to discuss your dietary needs. A good option for a first date is a local café where you can meet initially just for a drink and a chat. Or meet at a local National Trust garden or go for a walk.

- **Embracing our differences** – So far, my allergies have not been a problem when meeting new men. It obviously does narrow the potential pool but that is often a good thing. We are attracted to people who are like us and share similar interests, but we also find our differences intriguing when there is that special connection.

- **It is difficult for people if they care about you,** worrying whether or not you might suffer anaphylaxis on their watch.

Dan Kelly of the *May-Contain* blog says this:

> *"When I set out to create May-Contain there wasn't much content aimed at teenagers dating with an allergy. Since talking about it online, the number of people who have reached out to me has been overwhelming! My best piece of advice is always to be yourself and never hold back from telling your date about your allergy. I usually make a joke about it when I bring it up in conversation!"*

Allergic Living, gives advice on dating in a really insightful article on their website: **allergicliving.com**

Here are a few examples:

> *"A young woman called Tessa shares how she fell for a boy at university and always made sure her allergies were her problem. She managed it and didn't make a big thing about it in their relationship, preferring to stay away from the subject. She felt comforted to hear that her date's mother and sister both also had allergies, so thought this new guy would understand. He called off the relationship after three months stating the reason being that he didn't want to have to worry about her allergies all the time. A tough thing to hear and very upsetting for Tessa."*
>
> Tessa, Allergic Living dating article

> *One young guy called Dylan found added complications when drinking in bars and clubs. His allergies to tree nuts and peanuts meant he frequently had to turn away from girls who were leaning in to kiss him; he feels this may often put women off, but he couldn't take that risk without knowing what they'd eaten that night. In the heat of the moment those important conversations are not easy to have on the spot. He says: 'You can't make that move as you don't know what she's eaten.'"*

Sloane Miller, a New York-based psychotherapist who specialises in food allergy management, and author of *Allergic Girl: adventures in living well with food allergies*, reminds singles of the importance of 'the talk,' and that it doesn't need to be a big sit-down lecture. "There will be a natural opening in a conversation to bring up your needs in a chill way," says Miller, who is severely allergic to tree nuts and salmon, and also has allergies to several fruits and vegetables. "All you need to do is look for it, and if you don't see it, then you can create it."

They might not really understand

I have had some interesting responses to telling people that I could get anaphylaxis from nuts or dairy. Here are just a few:

"WOW! So, I could totally kill you on a date by slipping nuts in your meal and you'd never know"

– Yes, he did actually say this! Swift exit by me after that date.

"I could never give up eating nuts."

"Yeah, but how bad is it really?
You can eat some, like crumbs or something right?"

"So, basically, you can't eat ANYTHING then!"

"Well actually your dry skin didn't really bother me that much."

– Gee thanks for mentioning it!

Anyone who starts out early, listing your imperfections, will probably be hard work.

These kinds of comments may be made in jest, but I can never relax afterwards. Tune into the tell-tale signs that they do not really get it. You deserve better, you deserve someone who loves you and your differences.

Kissing with allergies

You might think that a cheeky kiss is harmless enough, but studies have shown that peanut allergen protein in particular – more so than other allergens – can remain in the saliva for quite some time. If your date has been munching away on a bag of peanuts before meeting you, this could be enough to cause a serious allergic reaction.

A study by The Food Allergy Institute from Mount Sinai School of Medicine, in New York, USA, showed that significant levels of peanut protein remained in saliva for over an hour after consumption. Interventions such as rinsing, brushing teeth and chewing gum, reduced the protein present but it still posed significant risk.

And according to New York allergist Dr Scott Sicherer, a study in 2006 suggests that between 5 per cent and 12 per cent of allergic individuals will experience a reaction from kissing someone who has eaten nuts. Sicherer and his colleagues had non-allergic participants eat peanut butter and then tested to see how much of the allergen remained in their saliva after activities such as rinsing, brushing or chewing gum. The results indicate that the best strategy is to avoid the allergen for several hours and have an allergen-free meal before starting to kiss.

My peanut allergy kiss

This has happened to me, leaving me with half my face swollen, but luckily no further reactions. It was embarrassing, a total passion killer, and I just hid in my room with an ice pack. But it was a very important lesson to learn early on.

It might seem awkward and embarrassing to have to mention this 'before' the kiss, it is kind of presumptuous, but at the same time, it can be an ice breaker and a life saver!

Ideally, your date should avoid eating any of the allergens that affect you before meeting you and especially while with you.

Latex allergy and dating

With a latex allergy, you need to carry your own safe condoms. Skyn and Durex have latex-free alternatives and you should probably take responsibility for providing these so that you know you will be safe. There are other latex-free brands on the market. Look out for other sources of latex. Some mattresses are made from latex, some sex toys also contain rubber so be mindful if things are going down that route to make sure you check everything is safe.

Dairy allergy and dating

You might not expect condoms to contain dairy but most normal rubber condoms contain milk protein in the dusty powder coating. You need to make sure you buy some that are dairy free and the Skyn range mentioned above, which are latex free, are also dairy free. There are many vegan condoms out there so research the internet to find some that suit you and your partner.

What if things get serious?

If you meet someone that you really click with, they will love you despite your allergies and they will do everything they can to help and support you and keep you safe.

A few things they may need guidance on are as follows:

- **Gifts** – You can joke about this and talk about the worst and least appropriate gifts received. Someone who just did not think, gave me a milk chocolate fruit and nut bar as a gift. This was at work and many of us were given the same. It is not suitable for someone allergic to nuts and dairy. Your partner will need to learn how to check ingredients labels like a ninja and think outside the box when it comes to gifts. Tell them the particular chocolate brands that are okay for you, if they want to buy a chocolate lover safe chocolate, it just takes some research, planning and probably internet shopping. There are a few brands that are both nut and dairy free on the market including Plamil, Cocoa Libre, Nomo or D&D Chocolates. Some brands say they are dairy free but may also have 'may contain' warnings on packaging due to the manufacturing process. I never risk this as chocolate production lines are cleaned or flushed out with chocolate so there is always a chance of cross-contamination of the brand that also makes a nut variety, or milk chocolate. Stick to the nut-free factory brands mentioned above.

- **How to cook allergen free** – Go through all the ingredients with them. Explain things like checking packet mixes and condiments, reading labels and suggest some suitable meals they could cook that you know are simple and easy to create. Better still, give them an allergy-free cookbook if they are keen on cooking you a meal. It can be quite romantic to cook together, so you could join them in the kitchen and help them get to grips with cooking free-from before you set them loose alone. (See Chapter 9 for a list of cookbooks you can try.)

- **Skin care and perfumes** – You may be sensitive to certain perfumes, shampoos, conditioners, shower gels and face creams. Do not be shy about explaining this to them and make sure that you always take your own shampoo and shower gel just in case. You do not want to have a skin reaction whilst away from home. If you are sensitive to perfumes this can be a tricky one. You will have to ask them if they wear fragrances and if you plan to visit their home, whether they use plug in fragrance devices. You may want to avoid certain places on a date if you are very sensitive to fragrances as anyone could be wearing perfume.

- **The bedroom** – If you are allergic to biological washing powder you might even need to discuss how they wash their clothes and bedding. This seems over the top, but you do not want to be itchy and uncomfortable all night. If they really like you, they won't mind you asking. It is a simple fix to remedy this.

- **Dusting and hoovering** – If you are allergic to dust and dust mites you may also need to discuss general housework. If they live in a dusty house, you could offer to help clean it with them. Explain that you need to clean more often to avoid reactions to dust and exacerbating your asthma. Well controlled asthma is essential for anyone with a life-threatening allergy.

- **Allergic reactions and how to respond** – You will need to demonstrate early on how to administer your adrenaline. Explain where your Allergy Action plan is, and what they might need to do should the matter arise.

- **Pets!** – This can be a deal breaker. If you are allergic to dogs or cats and they are an animal lover, they are unlikely to be a good match for you. It is a discussion to have early on. Some dogs are less allergenic so it could be worth meeting the pet to see if it irritates your airways, or skin, but this might put an end to the relationship. You cannot expect them to get rid of their dog or cat. You can arrange to meet them with their pet to see if you are allergic and take things from there.

- **Avoiding dangerous places** – You are an expert in spotting potential dangers but be aware when dating that your date might not be. Places like pubs, clubs, cinemas, theatres and concert halls, can all be places where nuts are either provided free in bowls or served as snacks during intervals. The problem with nuts is that people wipe the salty dust residue on their clothes and are likely to have nut traces on their hands or lips. In the cinema and theatre for instance, chair arms can be covered in peanut traces and they will not be getting regularly cleaned. You will need to remind them not to indulge in the free bowls of nuts and hopefully avoiding them, and moving to a safe distance from them, will not be a problem. Or even avoiding these places altogether if you are very anxious about your allergies.

Finding the one...

It's not easy, but you need to embrace your allergies and look for a date who is willing to take an active part in keeping you safe. They don't need to have allergies themselves, but they do need to understand the severity and in the words of Brigit Jones: 'accept you just as you are.' You want to find someone willing and capable of booking a meal at a restaurant and going through the checks necessary to ensure you get a safe meal. You don't want everything to always be down to you to check, although a little last-minute check is always a good idea to ensure everything is in hand.

CHAPTER 12

HOW TO HELP FAMILY AND FRIENDS HELP YOU

You want people to know what they need to do to help you, but not make everything always about you and your allergies. It is a delicate balance and can be hard because if you are like me, you do not want to make a fuss, you just want to be treated normally and to be able to relax in good company.

If you have life-threatening allergies, there is always an element of 'always on guard', ready to check everything... it is hard work but essential if you are to stay safe. This is how you must live: like a spy on a military mission ensuring that the assassin does not have a chance to take aim.

- **Explain your allergies** – explain fully what you are allergic to and all the derivatives of the allergens that affect you, for example cow's milk derivatives – include milk, cheese, butter, cream, yogurt... and so on. I find it helps to provide a list, either in writing or by email, especially if you have multiple allergies. Family and friends can then refer to it if they are planning to do any catering for you.

- **Demonstrate your adrenaline injector** – it is a good idea to show friends and family how to administer your adrenaline. This should be repeated regularly so that they remember and have a chance to practise.

- **Joining groups** – the anaphylaxis community and social media groups can be really useful research tools for your friends and family. Recommend that they join these groups as volunteers. They will find out so much more by getting involved. Some groups also organise events for volunteers, for example, The Anaphylaxis Campaign. The inquisitive can read, share, ask questions and expand their knowledge without always having to ask you.

- **Get involved and help them** – by this I mean, go early and help with any food prep, volunteer to make a cake, supply the picnic or organise things. It is hard work but by being integral and getting involved, you can teach and educate them and also be there when food is being made. Go through ingredients, help to cook that meal. I find most of my friends love that I come early to help with meal prep! It is no good just turning up announcing that you cannot eat the prepared food.

- **Talk about mistakes and share them** – I have blogged about mistakes that me and my family have made, and I share these so that others can learn. You might not be a blogger but do not be too scared to share when things go wrong. Do not blame, do not get angry just explain what needs to happen in the future to prevent accidents. For example, when a bowl that contained nuts is refilled with plain crisps, it could contain nut traces. Or when confusion arises about what has been added to a recipe.

CHAPTER 13

THE PSYCHOLOGICAL IMPACT OF LIVING WITH ANAPHYLAXIS

I grew up in a family where we did not talk about our feelings or emotions. We pulled our socks up, dusted ourselves off and got on with life. We did not moan about feeling down or scared; we put on a brave face and we coped.

This has been empowering in many ways. It has taught me to be brave, to face my problems and find my own solutions. It has taught me strength to cope alone, but it also means that I lack any understanding of how to ask for help or even admit that I need help.

"There are people worse off than you." Whilst true, this does not help when you are floored with fear. I thought I was coping pretty well with my allergies. I kept myself safe. I had reactions but whilst unpleasant and scary, I survived. I was an intelligent grown woman; I knew what to do and I was doing fine. How wrong I was.

I went from feeling quite cool and blasé, to housebound and quaking with fear. These feelings crept up on me over a period of years as my reactions got steadily worse. So, what happened to tip me over the edge?

The American anaphylactic attack

It all started after a trip to America in September 2017. I assumed eating out there would be easy. America would be more advanced than us in little old England, right? Well that is not the case. USA allergen regulations only cover 8 allergens, which are milk, eggs, fish, shellfish, tree nuts, peanuts, wheat and soya, (in the UK, the 14 top allergens must be listed) and there are not really any laws covering food service establishments. Risk is always the customer's own.

To cut a long story short, I ate a gluten-free muffin in a small chain café in Palm Springs, California. I was told it was dairy free but in fact, it contained milk as an ingredient.

The reaction I had after this milk consumption was delayed. We sat in the restaurant for an hour and a half, since I was pretty certain I had eaten some dairy. I took antihistamines and had a puff on my inhaler, and I was fine. I could breathe okay. I had no hives. I decided it must have been a tiny amount and so we left the restaurant.

I managed to walk back to my hotel after 45 minutes of shopping, pottering and walking along streets in high temperatures above 30°C. It was not until I was alone in my hotel room that these symptoms appeared: I felt a little unwell and began vomiting, my face swelled up and I began suffering diarrhoea. Then I really started going downhill. The nightmares I have about how this could have played out still haunt me.

I tried to phone reception and failed, probably because I dialled the wrong number. The last thing I did after failing to get help on the phone was to WhatsApp my work colleagues. In my panic, I could not remember 911, the emergency number in the US. (Make sure you have this written down before travelling.)

I sent my colleagues this message...

HELP, I AM HAVING AN ANAPHYLACTIC REACTION

And they came running. I thank God for these people because they saved my life.

I had propped open my hotel room door and administered both my adrenaline autoinjectors before collapsing.

I remember hearing the paramedics in the room but could not respond. I do not remember anything else.

I was whisked to the nearest hospital A&E by ambulance where they saved my life, stabilised my condition, kept me in for about 4 hours and then discharged me.

After the reaction, I did speak to the restaurant at great length by email when I got back to England, but their view was, that whilst they were sorry I had had a reaction I took the risk. They did not have the packaging anymore and they would take no responsibility. They claimed they had told me it might have traces of dairy. I have witnesses who can confirm that they did not tell me that. And let us be clear, it did not have traces, milk was an ingredient... I would

NEVER have eaten the muffin had I known that. I can live without a muffin.

An attack in 2018 in a British pub where everything went wrong

The next time an even worse reaction took place was just a year later in November 2018, in a local pub in Hertfordshire. I was out with the same work colleagues as luck would have it. A catastrophic breakdown in understanding, communication, basic customer care and staff training resulted in yet another allergic reaction for me, when a meal containing so much dairy you could open a dairy farm was served to me with profuse delight as the 'special dairy-free meal chef had made me'. It was a salmon starter roulade that looked like it contained cheese. I sent it back but was told that it was fine and that it had been made especially for me.

This turned out not to be the case, it did contain dairy and after one mouthful I had another anaphylactic reaction.

This time I had hives spreading up my arms, chest and neck. I felt unwell, but I could breathe okay in the pub. My boss made the pub dial 999 but otherwise the staff basically hid themselves, panicking I'm sure. The paramedics arrived, took my blood pressure, assessed my breathing and the hives spreading over my body. They made me get up and as I walked to the ambulance the reaction hit me, like a sledgehammer.

I tried to tell the paramedics that walking was not a good idea, but they said it was fine, that I did not need my adrenaline. I was shaking uncontrollably from head to toe. At this point I was able to speak and was begging for my adrenaline. The paramedics said they did not think I needed it. I passed out in the ambulance and do not remember anything else until my friends were by my side in hospital. I later found out that I was vomiting in the ambulance.

Again, so much went wrong with the immediate care, but all the paramedics will tell me is that they followed their guidelines. I should have taken my adrenaline straight away. I could breathe, my airways were not constricted at all. Not until I moved, stood and walked, did it all go horribly wrong. **Never ever get up and walk**. Stay seated, stay calm. Insist on being carried or ask for a wheelchair.

NB: In December 2019, the Artichoke pub in Croxley Green, where the incident took place, was found negligent by the local trading standards authority and fined £23,000, although I was not paid any compensation personally. Not a penny of the fine is given to the person who had the allergic reaction, although it was reported that I received £170, I didn't. The money goes back to Trading Standards to help them enforce the law and educate more food service establishments.

The prosecution did go some way to helping me see things would change and hopefully prevent any further mistakes at that establishment.

HOW DID THESE NEAR-DEATH EXPERIENCES AFFECT MY MENTAL HEALTH?

These were two serious, life-threatening situations and it is no surprise that I could not just pick myself up and carry on. I was just getting by, but I was close to tears all the time, could not handle a simple request to go out to lunch. If someone asked, I would just walk into the loos and cry. I went to work, saw friends, but I was not talking about what happened at the pub because when I tried to, I broke down in tears. I avoided social situations that involved any food. When I did venture out anywhere sociable, I had panic attacks and anxiety – it took me months to work out what was happening to me, because many of these attacks were completely unrelated to food. I also did not want to admit that I needed help.

To give you an example of an unrelated panic attack. I had been to London and had a successful 'reaction free meal' at a lovely restaurant near the Royal Albert Hall in Kensington. No mean feat and it had taken lots of planning and support from my lovely friends. However, when I came to leave to catch a tube to my brother's house just the other side of London, I was stuck. I was shaking, short of breath and unable to work out why. I now know I was having a panic attack which I found out later when I started having cognitive behavioural therapy (CBT) to help me deal with the trauma of the situation.

I found myself sitting on a doorstep in floods of uncontrollable tears with no idea how to navigate London, something I have been doing without a second thought for over 30 years. I had no idea how to get myself out of this situation. People just stared at me and walked past. No one stopped. Not one single person asked me if I was okay. I was walking in circles at one point trying to find the tube station and I just collapsed in the street and fell to my knees.

I managed to send a text message to my brother who phoned me, told me to book an Uber taxi to bring me to his house, and damn the expense. I did not really want to do this because all my family were there and would want to know all the details. I was just not in the mood to tell them. I just wanted to get home, but I did not know how to get home either. So, I booked an Uber and experienced the most traumatic taxi journey of my life. I'd booked an Uber pool taxi by mistake which picked up five people along the way, dropping them all off one by one, God knows where, while I wept into a soggy scarf in the back seat ignoring all questions. Some of my fellow passengers did ask if I was okay but I am ashamed to say I kind of ignored them because I could not speak properly. The taxi driver told me I would be okay; he'd get me to my brother's house.

When I got there, my brother had cleared a room and made me a nest with heaped up cushions on the sofa. He had a drink ready for me and told me to sit for a bit on my own, which was exactly what I needed. He gave me a huge hug and left me to collect my thoughts. I did sort myself out, by breathing deeply and telling myself I was okay. Then I spoke to the family, facing the inevitable 'but why couldn't you get a tube?', 'What happened to make you cry?', 'That taxi must have cost a fortune...' and so on...

I bumbled and mumbled and changed the subject and eventually we moved on. The tears kept leaking but I was able to slowly calm myself down. I did not know this was a panic attack at the time although I had heard of them before. It had just never happened to me. I was not that kind of person. I was not someone who had panic attacks. I was a strong independent woman.

Well not anymore it would seem!

Again, I ignored the signs that I needed help and buried my head in the sand. I did not talk to anyone. I could not, because every time I tried to, I began crying.

I stopped sleeping well, waking up in the night to see a black cloak coming down from the ceiling to cover me. I felt like I was awake but with a tremendous pressure on my chest holding me down, suffocating me and stopping me from getting up. I could not move, even an inch, and this weird pressure prevented me from crying out for help. I was sure I was awake when this happened which is a truly horrible experience.

I did not tell anyone about these dreams. I could not pass the first few sentences of this thing without breaking down in floods of tears. On the odd occasion that I tried to talk about it, I shut down, retreated, changed the subject, told the person I was okay and that I just needed time. What I actually needed was help.

Because of the nature of the most recent reactions to the pub meal and the seriousness of them, the local authorities began investigating because I had reported the restaurant to the Food Standards Agency (FSA). The authority then decided to take the pub to court and I was told not to discuss the impending court case, but I could have talked about my feelings without giving away any facts about times and places. Instead, I avoided the subject altogether so as not to say something that might jeopardise the case against the pub. Staying quiet compounded my misery: it was a dirty little secret I had to keep to myself.

LIVING WITH THE PSYCHOLOGICAL EFFECTS OF LIFE-THREATENING ALLERGIES

The psychological burden of living with life-threatening allergies for both parents, carers, children and adults is something that gets overlooked. The adrenaline is prescribed, and the patient is pretty much left to get on with it. For many this leaves a huge gap and an inability to process and live with the anxiety and fear.

For me, the psychological effect has been the hardest part of living with the multiple allergies that put my life at risk. Initially, I coped well, coasting along in a kind of blissful ignorance. I assumed an anaphylactic reaction would not happen to me. I was very careful, I did everything I could to stay safe, I educated myself, but I refused to miss out. I was probably a little blasé...

When I suffered a reaction to food, it was bad, but I remained conscious throughout the ordeal. I knew I would most likely recover but the physical pain of feeling that your throat has been held in a vice, the fear and worry of what had just happened and whether it would happen again, never really left me. I was becoming far more cautious and obsessed as my reactions began to change, to get more severe... I began to feel like my life really was in danger, and it was.

The worsening of my reactions had thrown me. I never thought I could die but I now realise it was a possibility. Because they were now very bad, I'd come to with hazy memories and none of them were good. Memories of begging to be saved. Snatches of frantic conversations between paramedics and hospital staff that I wish I had not heard, things like: 'Not responding...' and 'She's not going to die on my watch!'

My usual coping mechanisms crashed.

I finally realised I could not cope at all. Knowing I might die, I sought help, was lucky and found what I needed.

I stress that I am not qualified to advise anyone about treatment, but I can share my research and what I found invaluable to me.

So how and where do you go to get help with the psychological impact?

If you think you need help with anxiety, panic attacks or crippling fear, I advise you speak to your doctor or allergy specialist. This was the first step for me towards getting the help I needed.

I stress here that we are all different and what helped me may not help you. I tried many different things to see what would work and to find what would let me feel more in control and less like I was on the edge of the next panic attack. I am really lucky to have found lots of things that help, but also many things that just did not.

There are so many little things that I did after the initial few months of just hiding away and keeping myself safe. I had to hide, to make my world small, so I could come to terms with this 'thing' and take back control. And I did take back control. Admitting you need help is probably the hardest but the most important step.

After I had been through CBT counselling and explored a lot of different techniques and tools, all the little changes I made to my life made me much stronger.

Here are my top tips to help you cope with the emotional burden of living with a life-threatening allergy:

Step One — Speak to your GP

If you suffer with depression, anxiety, panic attacks or feel out of control and like you cannot cope with your emotions, speak to your GP and your allergy doctor.

I consulted my doctor about my weird scary dreams and discovered that you can wake during the period of sleep when you are partially paralysed. It is what stops most of us sleep walking, but it is not normal to wake up during this time in your sleep pattern and very frightening when you do. I learnt some breathing techniques to get me through these half-asleep, half-awake panic attacks. Once I knew I was safe, that it was just my weird body giving me yet another strange experience and challenge, it slowly began to happen less until eventually it stopped altogether.

My doctor told me that I could self-refer myself to Healthy Minds, the free, localised NHS service for people over 18 who need help with depression, anxiety and stress. This was the best advice he gave me.

Step Two — Speak to a trusted friend or colleague

If you feel you cannot talk to your GP, speak to someone. Find a trusted friend or colleague. You may have access to an employee advice line at work so call them. It can be difficult to speak to someone at first, but it is a step you need to take. You will probably be pleasantly surprised by how understanding and kind people are. We tell ourselves that we are useless and pathetic, but this just is not the case. We all deserve to get the help we need.

Step Three — Counselling referrals

I was lucky to be told about Healthy Minds but there are a number of programmes that offer similar services. You just need to find out what is available in your area. Ask your doctor to refer you and insist on being taken seriously.

Healthy Minds is an online self-referral service. I was lucky to get through to treatment in a few months. I filled in an online survey, answered lots of questions, and because I said I was fearing death daily, I was highlighted as needing swift help. I had one long and traumatic telephone interview during which they assessed what care I needed. After being accepted by Healthy Minds, I embarked on a 10-week group session course followed by one-to-one sessions. The course focused on anyone dealing with difficult emotions like anxiety, fear, panic attacks, pain management and accepting difficult medical diagnoses.

I found the latter much more helpful, but I did get a lot from the group sessions too. Though these were awful, scary and very emotional, they were worth it, and I learnt so much about myself and the strength of the others in the group.

Group therapy and why it works – There were about 12 of us to start. By the end, about six of us were still attending.

These mixed gender sessions are for people suffering with anxiety, stress and depression, and are not just for people with life-threatening allergies. We came from varied backgrounds with completely different experiences and journeys. For example, one lady had been diagnosed with multiple sclerosis, an incurable degenerative condition that affects your brain and spinal cord. Understandably, she was struggling with losing her independence and previously active life. Another lady had Lupus, an autoimmune disease that affects your body's systems including blood cells, brain, heart, lungs and kidneys. She struggled with pain management and juggling work, physical health and mental health. Another needed help coping with extreme anxiety, another with the pain from a serious injury that meant he could not work.

As I got to know this diverse group of amazing people, they helped me to understand that what I was experiencing was completely normal. It was okay, and indeed completely natural to feel these emotions. I had so many feelings and anxieties in common with this group of people who I had never met before. It made me realise that as humans, we are complex but also have so much in common. Most of all, I was not alone.

Each session lasted a couple of hours and drained me both physically and mentally. I would leave feeling absolutely exhausted, but they did help me a great deal. The only problem was the speed with which we moved from one session to the next. I never felt I grasped one concept properly before we moved to another. I struggled to keep up, but I could see the benefit of trying.

The sessions covered the following:

Session One — The first session involved introducing ourselves and hearing each other's stories. Everyone in the group, including the facilitators, were so kind and had never realised how serious allergies could be, and how life-limiting. They all said they could never live with such restrictions. I, in turn, felt huge empathy for them, for the things they could not do and the challenges they faced.

Session Two — Setting the course direction. Using mindfulness to work out what and how we responded to our symptoms. What did we do to cope with our anxiety and fear? For example, drinking, over-eating, taking medication and taking recreational drugs. We looked at difficult thoughts and emotions. I realised that I almost always got itchy and scratched my eczema when I became anxious – confirming the link to stress and skin conditions.

Session Three — Learning new ways to cope with symptoms. Acceptance and looking at our life and its values. Understanding what is important is a tough one for me. I struggled to pin it down. This could be your religion or a strong faith. A need to help others or a mission to live your life in a particular way.

Session Four — Goals, actions and problem solving. Stepping back from your thoughts. Mindful living: for example, brushing your teeth carefully, methodically, slowing right down. Looking at the times when I became anxious and examining how I could have responded to a situation in a more helpful way.

Session Five — Acceptance and mindfulness and looking at activity management. What activities can help manage your symptoms? This included the things we should do more of but often failed to make the time for. Looking at ourselves in a non-judgemental way and allowing ourselves time and space to work out what helped and what did not.

Session Six — Improving sleep. What is normal sleep? Keeping a sleep diary and setting goals to help improve sleep. I was encouraged to look at my sleep environment and work at improving it, putting in place good sleep management and a regime that would set me up for a good night's sleep.

Session Seven — Managing relationships and assertive communication. Asking for support, knowing who to speak to for the most constructive support. Using 'I' statements to avoid blame and how to speak to others in a non-judgemental way about my feelings. For example, saying things like: "When you laugh about people being vegan, or 'special needs' and make fun of my condition it really makes me feel upset, belittled and excluded..." Rather than flying in with accusations and snapping at someone. This really helped me with relationships at work where things were dealt with using the usual office banter. No one realised that this was upsetting me, and it really helped us all develop respectful boundaries in how we spoke about my allergies in the workplace.

Session Eight — Maintaining progress and managing setbacks. Goals, planning action, ongoing self-care. Self-encouragement and reality statements. Making plans to move forward. I was actually really worried about how I would cope when the course ended, but I talked it through, and I did cope.

This group therapy did help, but it also felt like a rollercoaster ride with no time to stop, learn and understand what we were being taught. It was one thing after another, and I struggled with some of the sessions. It was also quite traumatic breaking down in tears regularly in front of the group. I cried more than anyone else, but it gave me so much more understanding into their conditions, that we all suffer in different ways, experience pain and anxiety, so we are never alone.

One-to-one cognitive behavioural therapy (CBT)

CBT focuses on challenging unhelpful thoughts and behaviours that may have built up because of your anxieties around anaphylaxis. During CBT, a therapist will actively work with you to find unhealthy thought patterns, and work out how they may be causing self-destructive behaviours and beliefs. Once I completed the group session, I was eligible for CBT counselling if I was interested and I requested this straight away. I did have to wait a while for a suitable time and date, but I found these sessions the most useful.

They were hard. Initially, I found it very difficult to open up in counselling and it took a few sessions to even feel like we were getting started, but they were so helpful.

Each week we tackled something different and there was homework to do. The modules included the following:

Building Self-Compassion – Understanding self-compassion
This was a hard module for me. I could not say one nice thing about myself, which shocked me and made me cry just trying. It was difficult to realise that it was me that was being so hard on myself. No one else. I was actually being a complete bitch to myself and giving myself no compassion at all.

Building Self-Compassion – Barriers to self-compassion
Why does a seemingly intelligent individual have so many barriers in place preventing any self-compassion? I wanted everyone else to experience kindness and was almost crippled with empathy for others but had none left for myself. I had a long way to go but this self-compassion stuff sounded warming and soothing.

Building Self-Compassion – Preparing for self-compassion
This is about being attentive to how you feel, what is happening and why. It involved breathing techniques, practise and keeping a diary. Being a writer, I loved this kind of homework.

Compassionate Imagery

Trying to conjure up one image that signified compassion for me was almost impossible, but it also looked at giving compassion to others and how that might look. What I might say to a friend who asked me for advice or needed my help, then imagining saying those kind things to myself. When I hear those words spoken by me to me, I wonder where this meanness to myself came from? How it became normal to be so unkind and uncaring.

Self-Compassionate Thinking

Again, this involved keeping a diary of compassionate thoughts, so I was good at the journaling aspect of this homework. It also involved me writing a letter to myself which was surprisingly helpful and eye-opening. It also brought in gratitude and focus on the many positives.

Self-Compassionate Behaviour

I was beginning to love this counselling now. Learning how to take care of myself and learning that it is okay to be self-indulgent and selfish. Learning to set boundaries and say no. It also looked at caring for others, building compassion and looking at how you can cope with the day to day. It was empowering, learning that I really did deserve better and that I deserved respect.

Self-Compassionate Living

We talked about self-criticism and self-kindness, understanding both and working on building the latter into daily life. Understanding the self-compassion cycle and working on a maintenance plan that would help me continue to learn and build on the positive steps I had made.

How to Prevent a Relapse

I was feeling fearful that I would slide backwards when the sessions ended. I felt attached to my counsellor and did not know what I would do without her. This final session gave me constructive ideas on how to prevent this happening and what to do if I felt I was slipping back into old ways.

There was also a peer support group once the sessions had ended. Sadly, I never went to these, I just didn't have the courage. I wish I had done at the time but feel I'm alright now. Writing this book was therapy itself.

Other treatments for anxiety and fear

As well as CBT there are other treatments available including:

Medication – Various anti-anxiety and depression medications can help with managing your anxiety, fear or depression. Discuss them with your GP.

Support groups – Speak to your doctor or visit your library or local citizens advice bureau for guidance in locating these.

Local charities such as Mind – Contact your local Mind office to ask about counselling. Visit **mind.org.uk**

Mental Health Foundation – You can visit their website to find loads of resources, advice and help at **mentalhealth.org.uk**

Anxiety UK – is a charity that focuses on helping people living with anxiety. Visit **anxietyuk.org.uk**

Samaritans support – if you feel you have no one to talk to and cannot go to your doctor, there is always the Samaritans, a charity providing support to anyone suffering emotional distress. A trained supporter will always be at the end of a phone to listen to you 24 hours a day. Visit **samaritans.org** to find out more.

Call 111 to speak to the NHS – if you do not have a doctor, this free NHS helpline, manned by fully trained advisors, is available 24 hours a day. They will connect you to a nurse or doctor, give self-care advice or guidance on where to get help.

Step Four — Contact professional organisations

I phoned the Anaphylaxis Campaign helpline. It is useful to talk to someone non-judgemental about how you are. This was one of the first times I did open up and weep for about half an hour. The conversation helped immensely because for the first time, I was beginning to articulate how I felt, to speak about it and have someone listen and understand what I was going through.

They also have a professional contact on their books who has personal experience of anaphylaxis and can give counselling over the phone. In the end, I did not go down this route because the contact was very busy and could not fit me in for ages. I was able to get help through Healthy Minds faster. It is well worth a call to them though and they may be able to suggest other resources and people you can reach out to. They are able to provide one free session and you can decide whether to pay for further counselling.

Step Five — Speak to your friends and family

I still find this hard, but am slowly discovering I can discuss what happened to me without completely losing control. I am incredibly lucky to have an amazingly supportive family circle and close friends. Every one of them has been so helpful and has made great efforts to include me and not let me hide away from life. You know who you are!

Step Six — Do what you need to do to stay safe

For me, initially, this was hide away and lick my wounds. After my second near death experience, I hid in a cocoon and gently healed for at least three months. Enough time to grow in strength to get back out there.

Hiding away is not healthy in the long term. In the short term it made it easier for me to move forward. I only had to cope with the food I put on the table. I became very strict, did not go out, and refused invitations. The only place I felt safe was going to my Mum's for tea.

Step Seven — Use your creative talents to tap into your feelings

I think I am still healing and this process of documenting the journey I followed, getting it all down on paper, has been incredibly cathartic. I am not suggesting you all go out and write a book, but I cannot stress enough how important it is to find your creative outlet and use it to help healing. Whether it is speaking publicly, writing, drawing, painting or creating. This is also something you can do with your kids if they are the ones who have allergies.

We are all different, but I find often I can write down how I feel far more easily than I can say it out loud. Once I have opened the debate with myself and started to accept, analyse and move on, I find the talking part comes more easily. This is the same with other creative therapies.

Find out what works for you and use it, you might find a new passion or hobby that will help you express how you feel for the rest of your life. Doing creative activities – that do not involve any social media – where you have to immerse yourself, are good for your mental wellbeing. I even bought a colouring book for adults which I lose myself in for a happy half hour. It is both calming and rewarding and helps still my racing mind for a short time.

Step Eight — Review and update your action plan

I realised I needed to review my Action Plan and update it when it disintegrated into tiny pieces. Not much use to anyone.

Detail your symptoms, your reactions and your medication and what people need to do in case of anaphylaxis. Since my reactions have got much more serious, I need to stress the key things I have learned: that I need to take my adrenaline EVERY TIME I suffer anaphylaxis, and also the importance of not moving or walking at all while I am in shock.

Step Nine — Anger management

Why did I need anger management? I am not an angry person, but I found that I was raging at the world; so angry that this was happening to me, furious that I did not know how to get help and feeling like no one understood what I was going through.

My anger was spilling over into my work and personal life and I hated being an angry person. I was frightened that this strong emotion had started to take over my life. It led to jealousy of all those around me without a care in the world, just eating what they liked and not worrying about every tiny aspect of their day-to-day lives. I started to hate people for being so bloody happy with their biscuits, lunch, meals out... this had to stop. These were my friends.

Living with and managing anger is a complex area. The beginning of the journey is to accept your anger. To sit with it and talk to it. To understand where it is coming from. Think of it as an angry friend, just another emotion passing through. It is just trying to keep you safe. It can also be a very powerful emotion and I have learnt to channel mine into a burning passion to help, to do good, to change things. I still have moments of deep visceral anger at the world and myself for not managing to stay safe, but now I am in control of the anger and not the other way around.

I was recommended a book, *Taming a Powerful Emotion* by Gary Chapman, which gives some sensible techniques for moving forward from a better place: one of acceptance and understanding. I am sure there are many other resources out there, so go and explore, ask for help and learn how to turn your anger into a helpful tool. It is better than feeling nothing at all! When this happens, things are much harder to work with. If you are feeling angry, and cannot handle your anger, please do seek advice from your GP.

I am not a counsellor or specialist in helping people deal with anger, but here are the key messages I took from my CBT sessions, my reading, and my own research.

The acronym, SAIN, is a really good way of explaining the process. It stands for Stop, Allow, Investigate and Non-Identification.

- **Stop** – Think about where your anger is coming from. What caused it? Who are you angry with and why? This will help you work out how to deal with it.

- **Allow** – Just sit with your anger. Try to breathe deeply and allow the emotion to be there without taking any action. For me, this meant not contacting the pub to rant and rave and scream at them. Once you've accepted things, now you can think about what happens next.

- **Investigate** – This is self-explanatory, but it is important to learn from mistakes. What happened is done and the clock cannot be turned back, but what did you learn from the experience? Was there anything you could have done differently? Were there any external factors affecting what happened such as being stressed, or were you suffering a lack of sleep.

- **Non-Identification** – This is the most important part of the process. You are not your anger or your allergies. Something happened that was out of your control, mistakes were made, and you became ill. By letting feelings and thoughts go you should begin to find release.

One other thing I did on the recommendation of a good Instagram friend, Nathalie **@intolerantgourmand**, was to burn my anger! I wrote a letter to the restaurant, to the people who made me feel angry, to my body for putting me through all this and I poured out all my horrible feelings, thoughts and negativity. I didn't send these letters, I then put them all into a metal bin and burnt them. Go outside and do this safely or your home will be full of smoke!

The above steps can be used to work through any strong emotion that you are not comfortable with such as anxiety, fear and jealousy.

I also discovered this lovely quote from Tenzin Palmo, an author and Tibetan Buddhist, which neatly summarises this concept. Rather serendipitously, she featured in one of my Calm app mindful meditations.

> "*We're normally caught up in the current of our thinking, feeling and emotions. With awareness we can observe it all without being swept away.*"
>
> Tenzin Palmo

Step Ten — Read and listen

I am a voracious reader and found many books and articles to read about the psychological impact of life-threatening allergies. All of these helped me to come to terms with things slowly and in my own way. Now I'm a bit of a nerd so I read proper medical publications as well as blogs from others who've been there. I would warn against too much difficult reading as it can also trigger more anxiety, but for me it helped to know I was not alone, that others felt the same and that it was okay to be struggling with it.

I researched how people coped after accidents such as losing a limb, or losing sight, or receiving the diagnosis of cancer. I can't now recall exactly what I read but much of this awareness came from podcasts such as broadcaster Fearne Cotton's **Happy Place,** which invites inspirational guests who've been through difficult experiences to explore what makes them happy. Anything life-changing can teach you so much about yourself. I found a great sense of empathy, healing and strength from hearing how others coped in different situations with positivity, strength and bravery.

Here are two books that gave me extra insight.

Living with Allergies **by Emma Amoscato** – Everyone should read this one-stop-shop for anyone with allergies. Emma has two children who have life-threatening allergies and she has pulled together many personal anecdotes from people living with allergies.

I am, I am, I am, **by Maggie O'Farrell** – This book is a beautifully written memoir exploring the author Maggie O'Farrell's 17 brushes with death. It sounds a bit miserable describing it like that, but it is not. Maggie explains how she learnt from each experience; one chapter which stood out looked at her young daughter, who has a severe nut allergy, having an anaphylactic attack and Maggie's experience of having to rush her to hospital, and how she dealt with facing the prospect of the death of her child to anaphylaxis. I found this chapter so moving; it really helped me to learn how another woman coped seeing her own daughter in the same situation.

Step Eleven — Self-care and compassion

I have said this before, but I cannot stress it enough. Be kind to yourself. You are dealing with a lot of stress and need to take extra precautions to stay safe, but you need to feed your soul by allowing yourself time to rest and relax. Self-care is a hard one to master when you are someone who feels they must constantly be doing, helping, achieving and working. You may think that taking a break is laziness. On the contrary, learning what love, what nurturing and what compassion your body needs daily, is one of the best parts of recovery.

Think about how you can do the following, without judgement and completely in the moment.

- Just to do nothing but enjoy the view
- Have a long soak in a bath with your favourite bath oils
- Go for long walks
- Book a massage
- Call a good friend
- Sit down with a good book
- Anything that promotes rest, relaxation and healing

This is so important to your daily routine and yes, I mean daily. There should be some self-care every day. Look after yourself like you do others. I have been terrible at this, leaving my own desires and time to the very last and often failing to tend to my needs at all. I am now an expert in self-care and compassion. Because of this, I am more and more able to cope with the stress and challenges of living with allergies and I am a much nicer person. You may need to learn to say no to some things, things that do not nourish and nurture you. If you are doing things you really do not want to do, start to examine this. Are these things you can begin to retreat from? Surround yourself with people who build you up, not pull you down and drain your energies.

Step Twelve – Yoga

Restorative yoga allowed me to spend an hour just being, relaxing and finding a calm place. It is a bit like meditation but you use props like bolsters, blocks, eye pillows and blankets to support your body in a nurturing, safe way. I wasn't convinced before I tried it, but I realised that I had never thought a pastime could be so passive, to just be. You don't have to always be active, doing, stretching and pushing your body. You can learn a lot from just listening and being still. It was so peaceful and calming and really helped with my anxiety.

Yin yoga is the opposite to restorative yoga. It is hard work and really challenged me in a different way. In Yin yoga you hold a posture for longer than in a normal yoga practice, with the idea being to breathe, sit in the moment, experience discomfort and be okay with it. Thoughts are often uncomfortable and that's fine. They pass, just as the ache in your joints will go away when you come out of the posture. It takes a lot of concentration and I find that I can now hold postures for longer, relax and go with it and allow discomfort to be there without fighting it. It's very powerful in so many ways, not just dealing with anxiety but also my eczema itch and letting it go rather than always scratching and responding.

Focus on the positives

You might be thinking that there is nothing good about having a life-threatening allergy or even multiple allergies, but for me this is not the case. I would much rather not have allergies of course. I do feel the loss, the burden and the fear, but at the same time I know that I am healthier as a direct result of having to take such an interest in the food I eat. It has encouraged me to learn to cook and I now really enjoy baking and experimenting in the kitchen. It has also taught me greater empathy and has introduced me to so many people who are in the same boat. It is a close knit, helpful, nurturing community and I have been helped so much by the friends I have met through the Anaphylaxis Campaign and allergy events I have attended. It has also driven me to reach out to share my experiences to help others, through my award-winning blog **whatallergy.com**, and through volunteering, campaigning and helping to spread awareness. If I can help just one person not feel so alone and grow in confidence, this is worth it. Remember, you are not alone!

I asked Rebecca Knibb, Reader at Aston University, Birmingham, for her contribution. Rebecca has completed a number of studies into stress, depression and anxiety amongst parents, children and latterly adults with allergies. She has written a paper on the subject published in the *Journal of Allergy*: *Quality of Life, Stress, and Mental Health in Parents of Children with Parentally Diagnosed Food Allergy Compared to Medically Diagnosed and Healthy Controls*.

Over to Rebecca...

> *My first job, after graduating from University, was to run a project looking at why people diagnosed themselves as having a food allergy or intolerance. I knew nothing about food allergy before I started, but the topic fascinated me, and I wrote my PhD on the subject. After graduating with my PhD and working in other areas as a post-doc, I went back to food allergy research when I got my first lecturing post. I went to a few food allergy conferences and met some clinicians who were really interested in the psychological aspects of food allergy and it grew from there. When I began in 1995, there was almost no*

work on the psychological impact of food allergy, and I was the only psychologist at conferences talking about how important it was. Over the last 25 years, I am really proud to see just how much interest and research there now is on this subject and that clinicians see it as an important aspect to consider in their interaction with patients.

Our research has shown that food allergy is associated with high levels of anxiety in many parents and children, and also in adults with food allergy, which then has an impact on their quality of life. Not all patients and families have high levels of anxiety or worry, and some manage very well and only feel more anxious on certain occasions or at certain times of their lives. The challenges of living with food allergy change over time and so does the level of anxiety and worry. One of the main factors driving anxiety seems to be the unpredictable nature of food allergy and the difficulty in always avoiding allergens. Food and eating is such an integral part of our lives, and eating is necessary for survival, so having a food allergy has an everyday impact that you don't see in other long-term conditions. Much of our research is cross-sectional though, which means we ask people about their anxiety at one point in time and don't follow them over time. Following people over time would help us to work out times in people's lives when food allergy has a greater impact and what factors help people cope with this. This is the type of research we are now planning in order to help people with their anxiety and worry and to manage better.

Adults have not been the focus of research as much as children and parents, however I have been doing some work with adults who have been diagnosed with anaphylaxis as an adult. We have found that they feel just as anxious and worried as newly diagnosed adolescents or parents of newly diagnosed children and this is having an impact on their quality of life. We have recently published a study where we interviewed adults who had been diagnosed with anaphylaxis to not just food, but to other triggers such as bee or wasp stings, or medication such as general anaesthetic. They talked about how frightening it was at first and then how frustrating it was to avoid things you never had to avoid before. They talked about how important it was to maintain control over their lives and that the support of their family and friends was very important. We have developed a questionnaire to measure quality of life in these patients and are in the process of testing that to make sure it is reliable. We hope to do more work with adults in the future.

My advice to people who are struggling with anxiety is, if you think you have a food allergy or intolerance, or your child has, I would advise you to see your GP and ask for a referral to an allergy clinic for testing. Many people think they have food allergy or intolerance for lots of good reasons but might not have this condition and might have something else entirely. So, it is important to have the right diagnosis and allergy clinicians are the best people to give you advice. The two allergy charities, The Anaphylaxis Campaign and Allergy UK also have a huge amount of excellent information on their websites that can be trusted as accurate and up to date. They also run local support groups and have a lot of material such as fact sheets, that can be downloaded for free. They also run helplines and issue product alerts when foods need to be recalled due to labelling errors."

CHAPTER 14

CHILDREN

Here is a letter written by clinical psychologist Dr Gretta Little who lives in Australia. She has a 10-year-old daughter who suffers anaphylaxis from bee stings. Gretta's moving words sum up the struggles she and her daughter face, particularly with her daughter's school.

Dr Gretta Little:

> "*I am a clinical psychologist and my daughter, who is 10 years old, is anaphylactic to bees and an unidentified insect. While I do at times worry about her, I don't let it get in the way of family activity, but this does require sometimes providing her with a great deal of reassurance in certain situations. My problem is that the school she attends, while they understand the need to have an EpiPen in close proximity, do not understand the level of fear my daughter has to manage when outside, and do not provide any reassurance. In fact, they are unaware of her experiencing fear.*

There is no way to control the environment for insect allergy other than to keep the child inside, which isn't realistic in life. My child has experienced anaphylaxis wearing long pants, and shoes, which is what little prevention we can help our insect sensitive children with.

She has been asked to sit directly onto grass, she has been left on outdoor excursions without anyone supervising her, when she tells me about these times she is clearly extremely frightened, and when I raise these events with the teacher they are minimised. Recently, on school grounds, she requested antihistamine. Her medical bag had run out and the teacher chose to inform me at the end of the day. This was unnecessary as I would have left work to bring it to her, but even worse, they have antihistamine in their first aid kit on site. My daughter refused to attend school the next day.

She also recently refused to attend school camp held in the bush. I tried very hard to help her attend. She and I visited the campsite together prior to the trip. Unfortunately, there was an unusual number of bees there and three flew in her face and she physically had to remove herself.

The teacher continually refers to me as needing reassurance, saying, 'it is a big step up for me', when in fact my daughter needs to feel safe and needs to feel that the adults who have a duty of care over her are aware of her fear and the potential danger to her life.

My daughter does not have PTSD but she does have some anxiety symptoms, exacerbated by the teachers' lack of awareness.

There is a great fear of dread and dying that comes with anaphylaxis, as my daughter and many of my adult friends with the condition, have confirmed. My daughter daily participates in outdoor activities, but it is with the knowledge that there is an adult there who is aware and can hold the fear."

Anaphylaxis can be terrifying for children

Kids understand and can cope with far more than some of us ever give them credit for. They are incredibly resilient and can begin to learn to take responsibility for their own safety from a fairly young age, obviously with help and guidance.

My nieces and nephew are confident about my allergies at the ages of 10 to 13. They are well aware what I cannot eat and relish telling me they would love to share their chocolate but sadly they cannot because: 'Auntie Ruth is allergic to milk and nuts.' Cheeky monkeys.

If your child has life-threatening allergies it is important to have open and honest dialogue with them, their siblings and their friends and also their friends' parents.

Education – Make sure they know what their allergens look like.

Help them understand how to avoid them and the possible dangers, for example at parties, school activities, cookery lessons, at friends' houses.

Communication – Talk to your child and create games to help them explain how they feel. For instance, you could have a box where they can write down anything that is bothering them and then once a week you take a look and discuss ways they might cope, overcome or face these problems or fears.

Bullying – Talk to them about bullying, which sadly has become more common. Allergy bullying can take a nasty turn though as kids often do not understand consequences as well as they should.

Allergies can kill and should be taken very seriously. Allergy bullying should be taken very seriously and escalated to teachers and head teachers, so that lessons can be learned at every level.

Emma Amoscato, author of *Living with Allergies* and the blog **freefromfarmhouse.co.uk**, and the mother of two children with food allergy and shares some negative experiences that happened at her son's school.

Emma Amoscato:

> *"We always try to focus on what our children can do, rather than what they can't, but we have had a few challenging situations in the last year. Unfortunately, you can't always control how other people will act or the messages children are being given at home.*
>
> *A child at my son's school threatened him with a nut and chased him across the playground. Thankfully, my son ran straight to a teacher, but it is obviously a very worrying thing to happen. Initially, the school did not take the incident as seriously as they should have. They have been very receptive to creating a comprehensive allergy*

policy to keep our children safe but as this was an unprecedented incident, they were not fully prepared. After speaking to them, they took action and new procedures were put in place.

We also had another experience when a child told my son he wasn't being invited to a birthday party because of his allergies. While this is not a life-threatening situation, it is hard for a young child to hear.

I believe education is key to stopping these things happening. The school now do an allergy awareness assembly every term and I am on the Parent Teacher Association (PTA) to make sure all events are inclusive.

It is also important to talk openly about these challenges with our children. We can't shield them from all the difficulties of living with allergies. We need to acknowledge and address their emotions or anxieties and help them build resilience. We encourage our children to talk openly about their allergies and explain that many people don't know as much about them as us and may be scared or confused. However, we also say that a true friend will be willing to learn how to keep them safe and included, and that's what they deserve.'"

READING FOR KIDS

There are loads of books for kids to help them understand their life-threatening allergies. These ones have very good reviews.

Nutley the Nut-Free Squirrel by **Stephanie Sorkin** – Nutley is an adorable squirrel who doesn't let his nut allergy slow him down. Join him on his journey to stay healthy with the help of his friends.

The Princess and the Peanut Allergy by **Wendy McClure**, illustrated by Tammie Lyon – The princess can eat nuts, but her friend can't – she learns how important it is to include her friend in her party plans.

The BugaBees; Friends with Food Allergies by **Amy Recob** – The story of eight best friends such as Beetle, Cricket and Butterfly, as they face their respective food allergies with positivity and poise.

Tom's Secret Agents: A Book About a Young Kid with a Food Allergy by **Jamie Waggott** – A great little book for those curious about allergies; including those that have them and those with a classmate, friend or family member with one. The story covers treatment and finishes with the importance of having an emergency bag close by.

You, Me & Food Allergies by **Emma Amoscato** – Educate and empower children with food allergies with the first illustrated non-fiction book backed by Allergy UK.

CHAPTER 15

UNDERSTANDING THE LEGAL SITUATION IN THE UK

The European Academy of Allergy and Clinical Immunology (EAACI) say that 17 million Europeans suffer from food allergies, with 3.5 million of them being less than 25 years of age. Worldwide, it is an epidemic that has risen to 1 billion in the last 60 years according to **anaphylaxis.org**. The UK has the highest incidences of allergy in the world with around 2 million people suffering.

The Anaphylaxis Campaign say: 'Recent studies put the rise at approximately three-fold in the last 20 years, giving the UK one of the highest rates of allergic disease in the world.'

The UK has the second largest number of children with allergies at between 5 per cent and 8 per cent, only a little less than Australia, the country with the highest incidences affecting 9 per cent of the population.

The phrase: 'There weren't allergies in my day', is often used by the older generation and certainly there were less allergies, but they have always been around. Asthma-like symptoms were described 3,500 years ago in an Egyptian manuscript called the Ebers Papyrus, a medical papyrus of herbal knowledge dating to around 1550 BC.

Bird's Custard powder is egg free and was invented in the 1800s. Mr Bird's wife had an egg allergy that made her life difficult and limited the food she could eat.

Allergies are more common now, but they are also far better understood, documented, diagnosed and reported. How many deaths have been attributed to asthma, or another outcome, when they could be triggered by an undiagnosed allergy?

We live in a world where allergies do seem to be on the rise and becoming far more common every year, but we also live in a world with more choice promising research and hope for the future. We may not see a cure for anaphylaxis in our lifetime, but we can hope.

THE ALLERGY LAWS IN THE UK

Consumer Protection Act 1987 – A customer suffering an adverse reaction to a caterer's product may also sue for compensation as a result of being sold a 'defective' product.

The Food Safety Act 1990 and the Food Safety Regulations 1995 (revised from 1st January 2006) – Require caterers to provide 'safe' food to their customers. Safe food includes allergen-free food if you have specifically been asked to provide allergen-free food.

EU Food Information for Consumers Regulation No. 1169/2011, December 13th, 2014 – States that food business establishments must provide details of any of the top 14 allergens either in written or verbal format.

Food Information Regulations 2014 – Requires all pre-packaged food to have the top 14 allergens labelled in bold.

Natasha's Law to protect allergy sufferers 2021 – Comes into effect in October 2021. Natasha's Law requires all pre-packed food to display full ingredient and allergen labelling. Legislation has been amended by the government and will apply to all food prepared and packed on the same premises from which it is sold.

Under current regulations, food made on the premises it is to be sold at, does not need to be labelled with allergens and customers are expected to ask staff for allergen information.

Fifteen-year-old Natasha died in July 2016 after eating a baguette from Pret a Manger which had sesame seeds – to which she was severely allergic – baked into the dough.

Following her death, an inquest was held which found that there was no specific allergen labelling on the packaging of the baguette. The Coroner also published a prevention of future deaths report which highlighted concerns including the inadequate labelling of allergens by Pret and the lack of a system for monitoring allergic reactions to their products.

'May Contain': precautionary allergen labelling (accidental contamination) –The regulations do not cover any accidental allergen contamination, although under the Food Safety Action and the

Consumer Protection Acts (see above), an allergic consumer would still have legal protection provided they had told the establishment about their allergy.

The Food Standards Agency (FSA) recommends that: 'Advisory labelling on possible cross-contamination with allergens should be justifiable only on the basis of a risk assessment applied to a responsibly managed operation. Warning labels should only be used where there is a demonstrable and significant risk of allergen.'

CHAPTER 16

RESOURCES AND REFERENCES

There are lots of charities, social media groups and online resources you can turn to for help and guidance. Try to look for official sources you can trust as there are many websites claiming to offer you a cure for allergies which will not help you at all. Start with the specialist foundations and charities and move on from there.

THE ANAPHYLAXIS CAMPAIGN

Their website has a Knowledge Base and lots of information, facts and guidance for you to read. If you need to talk to someone urgently, why not call them now?

National helpline available from Monday to Friday between 9am and 5pm. Tel: +44 (0) 1252 542029

info@anaphylaxis.org.uk anaphylaxis.org.uk

ALLERGY UK

A British medical charity dedicated to helping adults and children with their allergies.

allergyuk.org

ALLERGIC LIVING

An American magazine with topical, relevant and interesting articles. It is always up to date with an authoritative voice and I often find useful information here.

allergicliving.com

ALLERGY AND ANAPHYLAXIS AUSTRALIA

An Australian charity. Their mission is to listen, guide and educate Australians living with allergic disease. If you're in Australia, they have a freephone helpline: 1300 728 000

allergyfacts.org.au

THE BRITISH SOCIETY FOR ALLERGY AND CLINICAL IMMUNOLOGY (BSACI)

BSACI is the national, professional and academic society that represents the specialty of allergy at all levels. Its aim is to improve the management of allergies, and related diseases of the immune system, in the United Kingdom, through education, training and research.

bsaci.org

THE EUROPEAN ACADEMY OF ALLERGY AND CLINICAL IMMUNOLOGY (EAACI)

An association of clinicians, researchers and allied health professionals, dedicated to improving the health of people affected by allergic diseases.

eaaci.org

FOOD ALLERGY AND RESEARCH EDUCATION (FARE)

The largest allergy charity in the US for those with potentially life-threatening food allergies. They advocate research and provide resources, support and hope for the entire food allergy community.

foodallergy.org

NATASHA ALLERGY RESEARCH FOUNDATION (NARF)

Natasha's Foundation was set up to help and cure people with allergies. Natasha's Foundation fund and support pioneering allergy research, bringing the greatest scientific minds together working for cures and better medicine.

narf.org.uk

NATASHA'S CORONER'S REPORT TO PREVENT FUTURE DEATHS

https://www.judiciary.uk/wp-content/uploads/2018/10/Natasha-LAPEROUSE-2018-0279.pdf

NATIONAL INSTITUTE FOR HEALTH AND CARE EXCELLENCE (NICE)

Their guideline covers assessment and referral for anaphylaxis. NICE aims to improve the quality of care for people with suspected anaphylaxis by detailing the assessments that are needed and recommending referral to specialist allergy services.

nice.org.uk/guidance/cg134

WORLD ALLERGY ORGANISATION (WAO)

An international umbrella organisation whose members consist of 103 regional and national allergology and clinical immunology societies from around the world. They collaborate with member societies providing direct educational outreach programmes to nearly 100 countries around the globe.

worldallergy.org

FINDING YOUR LOCAL ALLERGY CLINIC AND MENTAL HEALTH SUPPORT SERVICE

THE BRITISH SOCIETY FOR ALLERGY AND CLINICAL IMMUNOLOGY (BSACI)

They have loads of resources, including a search tool to help you find your closest allergy service.

bsaci.org

ASTHMA AND ECZEMA

ASTHMA UK

Working to stop asthma attacks and, ultimately, cure asthma.

asthma.org.uk

BRITISH ASSOCIATION OF DERMATOLOGISTS

A charity focused on teaching, training and the research of dermatology. They work with the Department of Health, patient bodies and commissioners across the UK, advising on best practice and the provision of dermatology services.

bad.org.uk

ECZEMA OUTREACH SUPPORT

Scotland based, Chief Executive Officer Magali Redding helps families and children with eczema. Everyone at EOS is dedicated and passionate about supporting families and improving eczema services.

eos.org.uk

NATIONAL ECZEMA ASSOCIATION

The US charity for eczema and a great resource. They are very active on social media and are a really useful resource.

nationaleczema.org

NATIONAL ECZEMA SOCIETY

A charity for everyone affected by eczema providing information and advice for people living with eczema and their families. A nurse-supported helpline.

Helpline number is 0800 089 1122, open Monday to Friday between 10:00am and 4:00pm, not including Bank Holidays.

eczema.org

FREE-FROM AND COELIAC

COELIAC UK

The charity for anyone with coeliac disease. They have resources for sufferers, health professionals and food outlets.

coeliac.org.uk

FOODS MATTER

A fantastic resource for food allergy and intolerance, coeliac disease, free-from food and free from recipes.

foodsmatter.com

FREEFROM FOOD AWARDS (FFFA)

The UK's only industry awards for free-from food. Started in 2008 by FoodsMatter and FreeFrom Foods Matter to encourage innovation and celebrate excellence in the free-from food industry. The awards are entirely independent.

freefromfoodawards.co.uk

THE NATIONAL CENTER FOR BIOTECHNOLOGY INFORMATION (NCBI)

This website holds many resources, studies and research papers. If you like to analyse and get down to the detail and really learn about this

subject, you'll find loads here. Just search in the tool bar at the top.
ncbi.nlm.nih.gov

MENTAL HEALTH, ANXIETY

ANXIETY UK

A charity that focuses on helping people living with anxiety.
anxietyuk.org.uk

HEALTHY MINDS – NHS SELF-REFERRAL

Cognitive behavioural therapy (CBT), available free through the NHS by self-referral. Google Healthy Minds and your area and your local group will come up.

MENTAL HEALTH FOUNDATION

You can visit their website to find loads of resources, advice and help on anything to do with mental health.
mentalhealth.org.uk

MIND

The mental health charity.
mind.org.uk

NATIONAL HEALTH SERVICE (NHS)

Call 111 if you don't have a doctor and are not registered. This free helpline is available 24 hours a day and will be able to give you advice on where to get help.
nhs.uk/conditions/anaphylaxis

PATIENT ADVICE AND LIAISON SERVICE (PALS)

If you are unhappy or unsatisfied with the support and guidance you've received from your doctor or specialist, contact PALS.

nhs.uk/pals

SAMARITANS

If you feel you have no one to talk to and can't go to your doctor, there is always the Samaritans who offer emotional support. They are always there at the end of the phone to listen to you 24 hours a day.

samaritans.org

MEDICAL ID BANDS

ICE ID

A large range of emergency bracelets for young and old.

iceid.co.uk

MEDIBAND

Custom made or stock medical ID bands.

mediband.com/gb

MEDICALERT

There are loads of designs now from stylish to sporty and kids' options.

medicalert.org.uk

MEDICAL TAGS

Medical Tags have a range of ID tags, medical identity tags, medical jewellery, ID bracelets and necklaces, allertags, SOS talisman and medical watches.

medicaltags.co.uk

UNIVERSAL MEDICAL ID

Medical ID jewellery in crafted leather and precious metal.

universalmedicalid.co.uk

ADRENALINE INJECTORS

EMERADE

Request a trainer pen and sign up for reminders if you are prescribed an Emerade injector.

emerade-bausch.co.uk

EPIPEN

Request a trainer pen and sign up for reminders if you are prescribed an EpiPen.

epipen.co.uk

JEXT

Request a trainer pen and sign up for reminders if you are prescribed a Jext pen.

jext.co.uk

PODCASTS

I have discovered podcasts. There are loads! Listening to audio books and programmes has been such an eye opener for me and a real escape. You both learn and disappear in a wonderworld of the spoken word. I previously thought I did not have time for podcasts but now I am hooked. You can listen over breakfast, in the car, in the bath, while out walking... in many parts of the day you might otherwise waste on social media. Expand your world and nurture your soul.

These are just a few that I enjoy and learn from regularly.

- **Eat Allergy Safe** by Nina Modak – Looks at the challenges of living with allergies, and how to solve them.

- **The Itch Podcast** – An American podcast with great guests and explores allergies, asthma and immunology with Dr Payel Gupta, with Kortney (a real-life allergy girl) asking the questions.

- **Allergy Today** – Hosted by Quentin Howard, Ruth Holroyd (me) and Alice Rose, this podcast aims to normalise allergies, ask the questions everyone wants to ask and explore the world of allergies, eczema and asthma in a chatty, informal format.

- **Happy Place** by Fearne Cotton – A feel-good podcast where broadcaster Fearne interviews different guests to find out what makes them happy and how they maintain a healthy work/life balance.

- **The Calmer You** by Chloe Brotheridge – A brilliant podcast to gently help you find a calmer way of living. Chloe has expert guests on her podcast and offers free resources on her website **calmer-you.com**

- **The Anxiety Guy** – Gives a man's perspective and is also a good listen. Bite- sized episodes to help you manage this natural emotion.

- **May Contain** – Hosted by Dan Kelly, explores all areas of living with allergies with different guests each episode. Dan tackles tricky subjects, it's a fun light-hearted listen that breaks the stigma of serious allergies.

- **Owning it** by Caroline Foran – Anxiety Podcast delves into the murky world of anxiety and helps you climb back out. It's normal, it's okay and it's possible to live with it.

- Some other anxiety podcasts you could listen to include **The Overwhelmed Brain, Headspace** and **Untangled**.

All you need to do is find the podcast icon on your smart phone and have a play. Search for people and things you are interested in or want to learn about. There is a whole world out there and it's just waiting to be discovered.

You don't have to just listen to allergy podcasts. It can be a little overwhelming, so I listen to lots of mindfulness, anxiety and just plain funny ones like **Fortunately** with Jane and Fi. Sometimes it's just about escape and not about learning and improving.

There are also dramas available free as podcasts such as **Boom** and **Blackout**, if you love having stories read to you. Getting Audible (an audio book app for your phone) is one of the things I've done for myself as part of my self-care. If I'm not listening to podcasts, I'm listening to a drama on Audible, the ultimate luxury and escape and saves me dropping my real books in the bathwater!

ALLERGY BOOKS

Living with Allergies by Emma Amoscato – Everyone should read this one-stop-shop for anyone with allergies. Emma has two children who have life-threatening allergies and she has pulled together many personal anecdotes from people living with allergies.

Don't Kill the Birthday Girl by Sandra Beasley – A sufferer's witty, sobering account of living with life-threatening food allergies.

Allergic Girl, Adventures of living well with allergies by Sloane Miller – is a really fun but well written book of her journey and how she tackles her allergies positively.

I am, I am, I am, by Maggie O'Farrell – This book is a beautifully written memoir exploring Maggie's seventeen brushes with death. It sounds a bit miserable describing it like that, but it is not. Maggie explains how she learnt from each experience; one chapter which stood out looked at her young daughter having an anaphylactic attack. It's Maggie's experience of having to rush her to hospital, and how she dealt with facing the prospect of the death of her child to anaphylaxis. I found this chapter so moving; it really helped me to learn how another woman coped seeing her own daughter in the same situation.

When Every Bite Matters: One Teen's Journey with Food Allergies by Olivier Deldicque – A book about the struggles a 15-year-old faces with a history of severe food allergies, written with a positive and realistic attitude. This book is very scientifically sound about food allergies with helpful advice for children who suffer life-threatening reactions to foods and their parents.

READING FOR KIDS

The BugaBees; Friends with Food Allergies by Amy Recob – The story of eight best friends such as Beetle, Cricket and Butterfly, as they face their respective food allergies with positivity and poise.

Nutley the Nut-Free Squirrel by Stephanie Sorkin – Nutley is an adorable squirrel who doesn't let his nut allergy slow him down. Join him on his journey to stay healthy with the help of his friends.

The Princess and the Peanut Allergy by Wendy McClure – illustrated by Tammie Lyon. The princess can eat nuts, but her friend can't – she learns how important it is to include her friend in her party plans.

Tom's Secret Agents: A Book About a Young Kid with a Food Allergy by Jamie Waggott – A great little book for those curious about allergies; including those that have them and those with a classmate, friend or family member with one. The story covers treatment and finishes with the importance of having an emergency bag close by.

You, Me & Food Allergies by Emma Amoscato (Out July 2020) Educate and empower children with food allergies, with the first illustrated non-fiction book.Backed by Allergy UK.

COOKBOOKS

The Allergy-Free Family Cookbook by Fiona Heggie & Ellie Lux – has good reviews on Amazon. For anyone cooking for a family it looks like a good one to try.

Chocolate Treats by Nina Modak – Free from all the top 14 allergens. Nina has allergies herself and experimented in her own kitchen to come up with these brilliant recipes. If you have a sweet tooth this one's for you!

Cooking Allergy-Free by Jenna Short – The recipes look amazing and writing this has made me want to experiment more in my own kitchen, so I'll be exploring this one more.

Deliciously Ella, Deliciously Ella Every Day and *Deliciously Ella, The plant-based cookbook* all by Ella Woodward – now Mills. She has written loads of cookbooks, all plant based and her recipes look pretty good.

The Eczema Detox by Karen Fischer – This is a lovely cookbook and perfect for anyone who also has eczema in the mix. It is more than a cookbook and explores the different foods that can be good and bad for eczema skin.

How to Cook for Food Allergies by Lucinda Bruce-Gardyne – One of the first cookbooks I bought, it contains loads of really simple and easy to create recipes. It was also the book that taught me how to adapt other recipes to be safe.

Simply Italian, Simply Gluten Free by Anna Del Conte and Michelle Berriedale-Johnson – If you love Italian food, risottos and pastas, but can't eat wheat, this one is a must. I adore this book and have taken 3 or 4 recipes as regular go-to meals. They are quick, simple to understand and divine!

The Wheat & Dairy Free Cookbook by Terence Stamp and Elizabeth Buxton – This one is probably my most loved cookbook. I used to buy

Terence Stamp's wheat-free flour before Doves Farm came onto the scene.

These appear on many free-from listings.

Allergy-Free and Easy Cooking by Cybele Pascal (US book)
The Allergy-Free Pantry by Colette Martin (US book)
Eat Dairy Free by Alisa Fleming
The Gluten, Wheat & Dairy Free Cookbook by Antoinette Savill
The Kitchen Alchemists Cookbook by Frances Castelli

ALLERGY APPS

Current at the time of writing

Allergy Translations – Many people use Google Translate but you can also use apps to help you translate phrases whilst travelling. There are a few to choose from. I quite liked the Allergic Traveller app. If you travel a lot, it means you don't need to keep getting translation cards done for each country and language you require.

Eating out apps – One I have used is **Dine Pilot**, which helps you find restaurants near you. There are many other companies creating apps that are designed to help you eat out safely with allergies. All of these are in creation and early days, so look out for them over the coming months.

Emerade, EpiPen and Jext – all have apps. It's a great idea to sign up to these to help you stay up to date with expiry dates, shortages and to help you understand your injector fully. All the apps have demonstration videos so you can remind yourself and familiarise yourself with how they work.

Foodmaestro – Helps you scan products in the supermarket to check they're safe. You filter your allergens and personalise the app to suit your needs.

Glass Onion – Popular in many pubs and restaurants, it allows you to filter menus with your allergens. It works but isn't helpful at removing elements of a meal, for example, if you can eat the bacon and eggs but not the sausages and toast in a breakfast. Be aware of this as it can seem very limiting at first look. Always speak to a server as well to ensure you can get a safe meal. They will be able to help you work out which dishes can have items removed safely.

Recipe apps – There are lots of apps that can help you with recipe planning which allow you to filter out your allergens and search for specific meal types. **Yummly** allowed me to tag my allergens, filter the types of cuisine I enjoyed, add a 'dislikes' list and get a list of recipes I might like to try. With over 2 million recipes and 4.6k reviews of 4.5 star or above, it's a good one to try.

BULLYING

BULLYING AND FOOD ALLERGY: WHAT CAN ALLERGISTS DO?

Advice from the American College of Allergy, Asthma and Immunology
acaai.org/resources/connect/letters-editor/bullyingandfoodallergywhatcanallergistsdo

THE ANTI-BULLYING ALLIANCE

Runs Anti-Bullying Week in November and tackles the behaviours that leads to bullying.
anti-bullyingalliance.org.uk

THE ANTI BULLYING NETWORK

An independent charity that supports anti-bullying work in schools, offering training, consultancy and publications to help.
antibullying.net

ANTI-BULLYING PRO

Part of the charity The Diana Award, a legacy to Diana, Princess of Wales, they help young people and professionals stand up to bullying.
antibullyingpro.com

SCIENTIFIC PAPERS, TELEVISION AND NEWSPAPER ARTICLES

CHAPTER 3

Risk of anaphylaxis after vaccination in children and adults – (2016) Virtually all vaccines have the potential to trigger anaphylaxis
Journal of Allergy and Clinical Immunology
https://www.ncbi.nlm.nih.gov/pmc/articles/PMC4783279/

Fatal Anaphylaxis: Mortality Rate and Risk Factors
Journal of Allergy Clinical Immunology in Practise (2017)
Paul J. Turner, MD, PhD, Elina Jerschow, MD, Thisanayagam Umasunthar, MD, Robert Lin, MD, Dianne E. Campbell, MD, PhD, and Robert J. Boyle,
https://www.ncbi.nlm.nih.gov/pmc/articles/PMC5589409/

Trace Peanut Study (2017) BSACI
Conducted by various universities including Cambridge University's School of Clinical Medicine and the paediatric department at Imperial College London, aimed to understand how exercise

and sleep affected the outcome of exposure to an allergen. **food.gov.uk/news-alerts/news/peanut-allergies-affected-by-exercise-and-sleep-deprivation-new-study-finds**

Dying from a food allergy is less likely than being murdered
Imperial College London, by Sam Wong (2013)
https://www.imperial.ac.uk/news/136431/dying-from-food-allergy-less-likely/

Natasha Allergy Research Foundation
Aims to help and cure people with allergies. Natasha's Foundation will fund and support pioneering allergy research bringing the greatest scientific minds together working for cures and better medicine.
https://www.narf.org.uk/

CHAPTER 5

Guidance on Completing a Written Allergy and Anaphylaxis Emergency Plan
Official Journal of American Academy of Pediatrics (2020)
pediatrics.aappublications.org/content/139/3/e20164005

FARE – Food Allergy & Anaphylaxis Emergency Care Plan
foodallergy.org/resources/food-allergy-anaphylaxis-emergency-care-plan

CHAPTER 7

Anaphylaxis Campaign Allergy Wise Adrenaline Auto-injector training
www.anaphylaxis.org.uk/information-training/allergywise-training

Anaphylaxis – how to use and store adrenaline
https://www.foodallergy.org/resources/anaphylaxis

CHAPTER 9

BBC1 Panorama. Takeaways fail to provide good allergen information. January 2019
https://www.telegraph.co.uk/news/2019/01/14/takeaways-failing-provide-correct-information-allergens-playing/

Bullying and Food Allergy: What Can Allergists Do?
acaai.org/resources/connect/letters-editor/bullyingandfoodallergywhatcanallergistsdo

Two thirds of takeaways still break the law
https://fdhospitality.com/advice/why-are-two-thirds-of-takeaways-still-breaking-the-law-on-allergy-information/

Bullying according to the journal Annals of Allergy, Asthma and Immunology
annallergy.org/article/S1081-1206(10)00733-7/abstract

CHAPTER 10

Single with Food Allergies: Advice on Dating and Relationships
https://www.allergicliving.com/2017/10/19/single-with-food-allergies-advice-on-dating-and-relationships/

Peanut allergen exposure through saliva: assessment and interventions to reduce exposure
https://www.ncbi.nlm.nih.gov/pubmed/16950293

J Allergy Clin Immunol. 2006 Sep;118(3):719-24. Epub 2006 Jul 24.

Translation Cards are available from the two main British allergy charities:
Anaphylaxis Campaign and Allergy UK
https://allergyaction.org/translations
allergyuk.org/get-help/translation-cards

Maloney JM, Chapman MD, Sicherer SH.

CHAPTER 14

EU Food Information for Consumers Regulation No. 1169/2011 - December 13th, 2014
https://eur-lex.europa.eu/legal-content/EN/ALL/?uri=CELEX%3A32011R1169

Packaging and Labelling Prepacked food - Food Information Regulations 2014
https://www.food.gov.uk/business-guidance/packaging-and-labelling

The Food Safety Act 1990
http://www.legislation.gov.uk/ukpga/1990/16/contents

Consumer Protection Act 1987
http://www.legislation.gov.uk/ukpga/1987/43/contents

'May Contain': precautionary allergen labelling
https://www.food.gov.uk/business-guidance/allergen-labelling-for-food-manufacturers

The Food Standards Agency (FSA)
https://www.food.gov.uk/food-safety

SCIENTIFIC PAPERS

Expert reaction to study on peanut allergy oral immunotherapy and allergic reactions. Research published in *The Lancet* demonstrates that immunotherapy for peanut allergies increased allergic reactions.
https://www.sciencemediacentre.org/expert-reaction-to-study-on-peanut-allergy-oral-immunotherapy-and-allergic-reactions/

Can Early Exposure Fix Food Allergies?
https://www.webmd.com/allergies/features/food-allergies-early-exposure#1

Guidance on Completing a Written Allergy and Anaphylaxis Emergency Plan
Julie Wang, Scott H. Sicherer, SECTION ON ALLERGY AND IMMUNOLOGY March 2017, VOLUME 139 / ISSUE 3
From the American Academy of Pediatrics

Clinical Report
pediatrics.aappublications.org/content/139/3/e20164005

Some really good points in this article about bullying.
One third of food allergic kids are bullied because of their allergy – American and Canadian Studies.
allergicliving.com/2018/05/15/food-allergy-bullying-how-to-spot-if-your-child-is-a-target-and-actions-to-take/

The psychosocial impact of life-threatening childhood food allergies.
ncbi.nlm.nih.gov/pubmed/23362632

The Anaphylaxis Campaign also has some good guidance on this subject in their Psychological Impact Factsheet: **anaphylaxis.org.uk/wp-content/uploads/2019/07/Anaphylaxis-Campaign-Psychological-Impact-Factsheet-2018.pdf**

One for parents of allergic kids,
Living with severe food allergy
thepsychologist.bps.org.uk/volume-27/edition-5/living-severe-food-allergy

The psychosocial impact of food allergy and food hypersensitivity in children, adolescents and their families: a review
https://onlinelibrary.wiley.com/doi/full/10.1111/j.1398-9995.2010.02342.x

Food Allergy and the Relationship with Mental Health, Quality of Life, and Self-Efficacy (2016)
Rebecca C. Knibb, Aaron Cortes, Christopher Barnes, and Carol Stalker.
https://www.ncbi.nlm.nih.gov/pmc/articles/PMC5027308/

The psychosocial impact of food allergy and food hypersensitivity in children, adolescents and their families: a review (2010)
A. J. Cummings R. C. Knibb R. M. King J. S. Lucas
https://onlinelibrary.wiley.com/doi/full/10.1111/j.1398-9995.2010.02342.x

Quality of Life, Stress, and Mental Health in Parents of Children with Parentally Diagnosed Food Allergy Compared to Medically Diagnosed and Healthy Controls
Gurkiran Birdi, Richard Cooke, and Rebecca Knibb*
https://www.ncbi.nlm.nih.gov/pmc/articles/PMC4939330/

Psychological burden of food allergy – (2007) **https://www.ncbi.nlm.nih.gov/pmc/articles/PMC4146781/**

Contributors

We would like to say a huge thank you to all our contributors for sharing their expertise in this area.

PROF. ADAM FOX

MD, MA(Hons), MSc, MB, BS, DCH, FRCPCH, FHEA, Dip Allergy

Professor of Paediatric Allergy at Allergy London

Professor in paediatric allergy at the private clinic Allergy London. Adam also spent 9 years as the clinical lead of allergy at Guy's and St Thomas' in London

@dradamfox allergylondon.com

Declarations of interest can be found at **http://www.whopaysthisdoctor.org/doctor/511**

DANIEL KELLY

Blogger at may-contain.com and the May Contain Podcast.

DR FRANCESCA SAWER

Highly Specialist Clinical Psychologist, Guy's and St Thomas' NHS Foundation Trust, Evelina Hospital Children's Allergy Service

Francesca is a Highly Specialist Clinical Psychologist who works full time in the NHS. She specialises in paediatric settings, working with children and families to support with the management of health conditions and neurodevelopmental disorders and the impact that these have on mental health and wellbeing. She currently works in the Children's Allergy Service at the Evelina Children's Hospital in London, which is one of only a handful of specialist psychology services to offer psychological support to children and young people living with allergies in the UK.

DR GRETTA LITTLE

Clinical psychologist at Helios Psychology, Perth, Western Australia.

Gretta approaches each client as an individual, tailoring interventions within their unique history and circumstances. Gretta works with children, adolescents, adults and older adults using cognitive behavioural, acceptance and commitment and schema therapies as well as applied behavioural analysis.

REBECCA KNIBB

Reader at Aston University

Rebecca is a Chartered Psychologist and practitioner Health Psychologist with 25 years of experience of conducting research into the psychological impact of allergies. She graduated from Birmingham University with a PhD in 1999 and more recently completed an MSc in Cognitive Behavioural Therapy.

TANYA EDNAN-LAPEROUSE

Founder of The Natasha Foundation

Tanya and her family set up Natasha's Foundation with a clear vision; to help and cure people with allergies. Natasha's Foundation will fund and support pioneering allergy research bringing the greatest scientific minds together working for cures and better medicine. **narf.org.uk**

EMMA AMOSCATO

Author of *Living with Allergies* and her new children's book *You, Me and Food Allergies.* freefromfarmhouse.co.uk

CLARE HUSSEIN

Mum of an allergic child.

You can find her on Instagram @south_coast_mum

THALINA HOUGHTON

Blogger at allergiesinbold.com

Acknowledgements

I would like firstly to thank Michelle Berriedale-Johnson and Sally Beck of Curlew Books for believing in me and giving me the chance to fulfil a lifelong ambition; to write a book about my emotional anaphylaxis journey.

Special thanks to everyone who helped me write this work, especially the wonderful experts, bloggers and allergy community who contributed their stories, views and expert advice. You can find out about them in the Contributors section.

I am doubly thrilled that it is a book that will be helpful to so many who are struggling with a diagnosis of life-threatening allergies. It makes the whole experience more special.

To my family, for understanding me and never judging, even when I was at my lowest points and probably being a complete pain in the backside. I am incredibly lucky to have a family who plan every single event with my safety in mind, and for that, I will always be eternally grateful.

My friends, particularly my oldest friends Fran, Becci and the two Karens, who continue to invite me to their dinner parties, despite me being difficult to cater for. And also, to Michelle, whose free-from spreads are legendary, and which I am always able to enjoy with no fear, and much appreciation.

Despite me being 'every chef's worst nightmare', these people continue to embrace my allergies and never make me feel that it is too much like hard work.

Thank you also to the chefs who do not think I am their worst nightmare. My favourite chefs Dominic Teague of One Alwdych, Chris Bridges, from the hotel Summergrove Halls in Carlisle, Heather Umlah who catered for a yoga retreat I loved and is a chef for sustainable events – prove that cooking free-from can be tasty and enjoyed by everyone.

And to my friends, who are almost too numerous to thank and count. I am forever thankful to Clare and Caroline for being with me during the last two very severe reactions and for saving my life through their swift action, and all my work colleagues who made me feel included and cooked me cakes and cookies. To all my newfound running community friends, who never mention my red, eczema skin, nor the fact that I always bring my own cake! And who now eat my cake as they have discovered that just because it is free-from, it is not lacking in taste!

Finally, to my therapist Lara who I never thought I would cope without, who gave me the insight, strength and time to discover who I really am and how much compassion I really deserve.

Thank you all for being kind to the allergic girl.